THE WATTS HISTORY OF SPORTS

hockey

A History of the Fastest Game on Ice

MARK STEWART

FRANKLIN WATTS
A Division of Grolier Publishing
New York • London • Hong Kong • Sydney
Danbury, Connecticut

Cover design by Dave Klaboe   Series design by Molly Heron
Photographs ©: AllSport USA: cover bottom left, 74, 75 (Mike Powell); AP/Wide World Photos: cover bottom right, 33, 38, 40, 57 bottom, 61, 91; Archive Photos: 77 (Reuters/Mike Blake), cover top right, cover center left, 45, 47; Brown Brothers: 32; Bruce Bennett Studios: 92 (Scott Levy), 83 (J. McIsaac), cover top left, 95 (Vin Pugliese), cover bottom center, 85 (Winklen), cover middle center, 16, 44, 50, 53, 63 right, 66, 70, 84, 96; Corbis-Bettmann: 6, 37, 59, 65 top, 76 (UPI), 10, 57 top, 71; Hockey Hall of Fame: 67 (Graphic Artists), 25, 39, 51 (Imperial Oil-Turofsky), 26 (James Rice), cover center right, 81 (Doug MacLellan), 64 (Frank Prazak), 11, 13, 14 bottom, 18, 23, 24, 28, 29, 34, 60; SportsChrome East/West: 88; Team Stewart, Inc.: 5 (Bufford Boston), 68 (Collier-MacMillan Canada, LTD.), 72 (Contemporary Book, Inc./Terry Jones), 69 (Hawthorn Books, Inc./Colleen Howe), 14 top (Illustrated Post Card Co., Montreal), cover top center, 36 (Prudential), 42 (Sport/McFadden Publications, Inc.), 52 (Sports Illustrated/Time Inc.), 56, 65 bottom (T.C.G.), 80 (The Hockey News), 63 left (The Sporting News), 48 right (York Hockey Album), 48 left.

Visit Franklin Watts on the Internet at:
http://publishing.grolier.com

Library of Congress Cataloging-in-Publication Data
Stewart, Mark
    Hockey: A history of the fastest game on ice/ Mark Stewart.
    p. cm. — (The Watts history of sports)
    Includes bibliographical references and index.
    Summary: Discusses the origins and evolution of the game of hockey,
        as well as memorable events and key personalities in the game's history.
    ISBN 0-531-11494-5
    1. Hockey—History—Juvenile literature.
    [1. Hockey—History.] I. Title II. Series.
    GV846.5.S74 1998
    796.962'09—dc21   98-25039
                                                                       CIP
                                                                       AC

CONTENTS

THE HISTORY OF HOCKEY

The Roots of the Game

When sports fans think about hockey, they usually think about Canada. And for good reason: The game in its present form flourished there more than 100 years ago and then spread throughout the world. Was the game born in Canada? That is a subject of considerable debate. None of the basics of hockey—the stick, the puck, the skate—came from Canada. And obviously the Canadians did not invent ice. In fact, the elements of the world's fastest sport came together over the centuries, from every corner of the globe. As a result, it is not entirely clear who invented hockey, where it was first played, or even how the game got its name.

Hockey is almost certainly the oldest stick-and-ball game known to man. In its most basic form, it appears to have been played in an organized manner for about 3,000 years, although not until much more recently was the game played on ice. In 1922, an ancient carving attributed to Themistocles was unearthed in Greece. It dated back to approximately 500 B.C., and it depicted men playing a hockeylike game with sticks. It even showed two combatants crouched in the face-off position. Archaeological evidence indicates that the Greeks borrowed this game from the Persians, who had already been playing it for quite some time.

When the Greek empire gave way to the rule of Rome, a form of field hockey was adopted by legionnaires and spread to the

HOCKEY ON THE ICE.

Ice hockey, a game offering respite from the cabin fever of frigid, long northern winters, developed and matured on Canada's frozen ponds and rivers and has been a national obsession in that country for more than a century.

far corners of the Roman world. For more than 500 years, field hockey disappeared from the historical record in Europe, although it was probably played during early medieval times in some form or another. We know this because the game was specifically outlawed in England for several hundred years. The royal family believed that hockey interfered with archery training, and archery was the country's national defense.

Field hockey reappeared in Europe during the 1400s in various forms, gaining popularity particularly in France and Britain. In the 1600s, an ice game similar to hockey, called *kolven,* was played in Holland. And people in the Scandinavian countries also appear to have been playing a hockeylike game.

Across the Atlantic, hockey had developed on its own and was thriving among the native cultures of North and Central America long before contact with Europeans. In 1740, French explorers in North America's St. Lawrence River Valley came upon a group of Iroquois playing a game with sticks and a ball on a frozen pond. The Frenchmen reported that whenever a player got smacked in the shins, he would yell, "Hogee!" which they later learned meant, "It hurts!" Is this the origin of the term *hockey?* No one can say for sure. The French word for the shepherd's crook sometimes used as a stick in early games is *hoquet.* Perhaps this is the root of the word. There are even those who believe hockey was named after 17th-century Dutch artist Romein de Hooghe, whose most famous painting depicted his countrymen skating on blades fashioned from animal bones and whacking a flat rock across a frozen canal.

Modern ice hockey claims as ancestors hockeylike games played by the Greeks, Romans, Dutch, English, Irish, and Native Americans, who played a stick-and-ball game both on grass—as these Cherokees did at a 1947 event—and on the ice.

An alternative theory is that hockey evolved from the Irish sport of hurling, which dates back many centuries—perhaps even back to Roman times. Those who support this claim point to the curved stick, which is called a *hurley*. Is this where the word *hockey* came from? Certainly the two games are similar. In ancient times, teams from two villages would meet on a field in what was probably a form of ritual warfare. Each man was armed with a curved tree branch with which he would attempt to balance a stone or a hardened cow dropping. The idea was to run down the field and then swat it into an opponent's goal, which was formed by bending two saplings together and tying them at the top. These early games were deadly serious; there is some indication that the losers were tortured or even executed for letting their fellow villagers down.

The curved stick was also the instrument of choice for *shinny,* a popular sport in Western Europe and England and later in North America. Shinny was actually an informal name for any hockeylike game and came from the fact that players were as likely to whack an opponent in the shins as they were to actually connect with the ball. A goal was scored when the ball was driven through a goal fashioned of stones placed four to six feet apart. At some point (an exact date and location has never been established), someone moved this game to the ice and replaced the ball with a block of wood.

When and where ice hockey first came to Canada is also a subject of much debate. As previously mentioned, the natives had been playing similar games for untold centuries, but the first Europeans to hit the ice might have been the British soldiers sent to North America to man English forts in the 1820s and 1830s. Most had probably seen shinny played on the ice back home, but none had ever been to a place where the winters were so frigid and long. To break the monotony and let loose some of their pent-up energy, the soldiers would gather outside the garrison and engage in an hour or so of disorganized mayhem. The local settlers no doubt watched them with great amusement and interest and eventually joined in the games.

Some believe that Canadian hockey began much earlier. Around 1810, some young men from King's College in Windsor, Nova Scotia, grabbed their hurleys and convened on a frozen stretch of water measuring roughly 200 feet by 50 feet. Many regard these contests, played on Long Pond, as the first hockey games.

Regardless of who introduced the sport to Canada, hockey games were regular occurrences by the 1840s. By the 1860s, when the first mass-produced ice skates became available, hockey started to challenge lacrosse as Canada's preeminent sport.

The Growth of Canadian Hockey

Ice hockey as played during the mid-19th century, was still years away from resembling the modern version of the sport. It was not unusual for teams to number 20 or 30 a side; and occasionally the lure of scoring became so great that a player would wheel around and send the puck skittering into his own goal, which was typically two big sticks jammed through holes in the ice. If a player batted the puck wide of the goal, it might go another hundred feet, and if a pass was missed, the puck would disappear into a snowbank.

ROYAL BEGINNINGS

In the winter of 1853—a particularly cold one in England—guests at a party held by the British royal family on the grounds of Windsor Castle decided to play field hockey on a frozen pond. Field hockey, in its modern form, was a relatively new sport, and thus was quite popular. Goals were set up and the ball was replaced by the bung from a barrel. The game was played by the royals and officers of the guard, with Queen Victoria and her attendants cheering from the side.

Despite claims to the contrary, this informal get-together technically marks the first time a game specifically called hockey was played on ice. Within a decade, hockey on ice had become fairly common in England. In fact, with the introduction of ice skates in the early 1860s, skating in general had become much more popular. Ironically, this might have killed hockey in England before it ever had a chance to take off. Recreational skaters quite understandably feared hockey games and hated having to share the ice with rowdy and sometimes drunken players. Columns urging that hockey be kept on the grass and off the ice appeared regularly in London newspapers, and the police were sometimes summoned to break up disorderly games. Ironically, the British royal family both played and supported the game, and when their European cousins came visiting, they were quick to introduce it to them.

During the 1890s, club hockey was played at London's Hengler Rink (*rink,* by the way, is a Scottish word), and there was almost always a royal presence in the stands. Despite everything going for the sport, ice hockey died out in England by World War I, pushed off the ice by those seeking a leisurely skate.

Some of the more organized games featured crudely fashioned sideboards, but the average 19th-century player never saw a proper rink in his lifetime.

The rules during this time differed from region to region, but three basic regulations were considered universal. First, play would be continuous, stopping only when the puck had to be retrieved. Second, a player could not switch teams during a match, no matter how badly his team was losing. And third, games would last until no one could play anymore, whether the cause was exhaustion, frozen fingers and toes, bad weather, or darkness. A fourth rule, which forbade forward passing, was not considered unusual or restrictive. Most contact sports of that time—including soccer and rugby—did not allow it.

As for equipment, it would be another 20 years before mass-produced hockey sticks would become available, so players

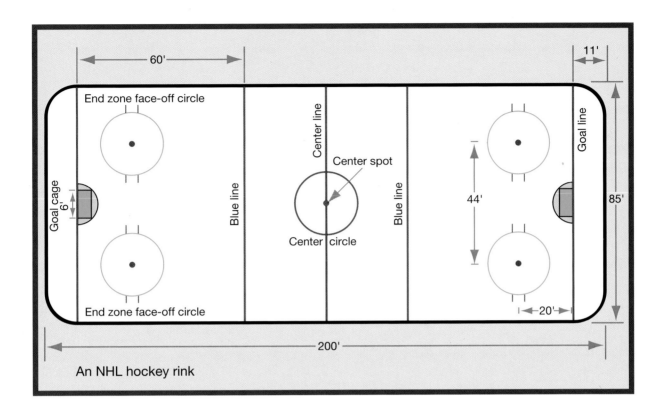

An NHL hockey rink

made their own, usually from tree branches. A well-formed, nicely balanced stick was a prized possession, and no doubt some enterprising souls made a few extra shillings producing sticks for local players. The puck, which got its name from the old English word for a little demon, could be anything from a rubber ball to a pinecone to a tin can. The popular choice for padding was old newspapers, which were lashed around the legs and arms with rope or twine. Goalies preferred to use out-of-date mail order catalogs for leg pads and began employing baseball chest protectors (ordered from those very same catalogs) once shooters learned how to lift the puck.

The first modern goal was the brainchild of a man named Francis Nelson, who got the idea while visiting a fishing village. He bought a length of net and strung it between two sticks jammed into the ice. Prior to that, most games required a goal judge, who would stand behind two rocks and wave a white handkerchief when he saw the puck cross the line. The net made this job obsolete, which was fine with the goal judges. Crowds tended to drink quite heavily to ward off the cold during these early matches, and a controversial call by a goal judge often invited a hail of snowballs and empty bottles. With the advent of the net, there could be little question as to whether the puck was in or out.

By the second half of the 19th century the roots of organized hockey were being established. In Kingston, a small city in the province of Ontario, the rowdy game played by British soldiers had developed into an organized league in the 1850s. A regiment called the Royal Canadian Rifles divided itself into several teams each winter and held games on the city's frozen harbor. As the population spread west across Canada, so too did military units, schools, social clubs, and sports clubs. Each had its own hockey team, and they played one another as often as possible. In the East, hockey teams began popping up from Quebec all the way north to Hudson Bay and out to the Atlantic Ocean.

In most regions, hockey was still played with few rules. In some places, though, the game was getting a bit more sophisticated. One such place was Halifax, Nova Scotia. A young man named J. G. A. Creighton grew up there playing a highly regimented form of hockey, and when he enrolled at Montreal's McGill University he was apparently appalled by the state of the game in the big city. Creighton undertook to organize a match between two groups of students, using the tighter rules he had learned back home. This game, played in 1879, is usually recognized as the first official hockey game, although there were some 60 players on the ice.

Soon, however, hockey would begin to resemble the modern game. A major step in that direction was taken in 1881, when two McGill students—W. F. Robertson and R. F. Smith—sat down and created a hockey rule book for play at the school. The inspiration had come from Robertson, who on a journey to England in 1879 witnessed a well-played field-hockey match. He became convinced that the same level of play could be achieved on the ice and determined that an ambitious set of regulations would have to be adopted. He and Smith borrowed from field hockey, lacrosse, soccer, and hurling to come up with these rules, the most important of which was limiting sides to nine players.

This had an instant impact on the game's popularity as it spread across Canada. Without the thundering herds of players that had formerly characterized hockey, individuals could showcase their skating and shooting skills, and spectators could actually see and appreciate them. Almost overnight, hockey went from a raucous, slashing melee to a game of skill, strategy, and organization.

In 1885, the first true hockey league was formed in Kingston, Ontario. It was a

By the late 19th century hockey had swept across Canada and begun to spread into the United States. The players in this illustration of an 1888 game in New Jersey are wearing roller skates, but otherwise the elements of the modern game are present.

The 1889 Rideau Rebels of Ottawa, a founding club in one of Canada's first organized hockey leagues and an athletic outlet for Ottawa's political elite, including two of Lord Stanley's sons—Arthur, standing second from left, and Edward, seated at far left.

four-team organization that included two school teams and two athletic clubs. That same year, in Montreal, the Amateur Hockey Association of Canada (AHA) was formed. It put three teams in Montreal, one in Ottawa, and a fifth in Quebec. The AHA also reduced team sizes to seven skaters—just one more than the modern six-on-six game. Teams typically had a goaltender and two defensemen, one of whom played near the goal and the other a bit up ice to meet onrushing attackers. Three forwards formed a front line while a rover zipped back and forth as play dictated.

Within a decade, several more leagues had sprung up across Canada; more than 100 clubs were active in the Montreal area alone. Political squabbles within the AHA led to its demise after the 1898 season, but in its place came the Canadian Amateur

USING MOTHER NATURE'S ICE

Top-level hockey was still played on natural ice in the 1890s, with grandstands built around the edges of frozen ponds or rivers. These structures could be quite large and elaborate, with some seating thousands of spectators. Many were covered and featured electric lights for night games. The season would usually begin just before Christmas and end sometime in March, so quite a few games had to be squeezed into a 15- or 16-week period. League games were usually played on Saturday evenings.

THE FIRST REFEREES

Playing hockey during the 19th century was nothing compared to being a hockey referee. Drunken fans and frustrated players regularly threatened officials, and for many years the host team had the right to remove a referee if he did not meet its approval. Although the metal whistle had been invented, it was of no use because in the frigid temperatures it would fuse to a person's lips. Instead, refs used cowbells to stop play. This idea was dreamed up by Fred Waghorne, perhaps the most respected official of his day.

Waghorne is also credited with inventing the face-off. Previously, the referee would lay the puck on the ice between two players, then bend over and grasp the ends of their sticks with his hands. He would maneuver the blades so they would rest against opposite sides of the puck, then move away quickly and yell, "Play!" In theory, this was a fine idea. In practice, it was not. Players rarely waited for the official go-ahead and sometimes began slashing away while the poor referee's hands were still on their sticks. Waghorne earned the enduring appreciation of his coworkers when, one day, he told the players to put their sticks on the ice 18 inches apart, then threw the puck in between them and darted away.

Hockey League, which remains Canada's most important amateur hockey organization to this day.

Enter the Stanley Cup

The most important development of the 1890s came in 1892, when Frederick Arthur, Lord Stanley of Preston, paid 10 guineas (about $50) for a lovely silver mug and announced that it would be awarded to the country's best amateur hockey team. In 1893, the Dominion Challenge Cup went to the regular-season champion of the Amateur Hockey Association, the Montreal Amateur Athletic Association team. The Montreal AAAs were led by Haviland Routh, who scored 12 goals in 7 games, and Billy Barlow, who chipped in with 7. Thereafter the trophy became known as the Stanley Cup.

Already Canada's favorite game, ice hockey reached an entirely new level of popularity thanks to this trophy. Whichever team possessed the Stanley Cup would be responsible for defending it against any and all legitimate challengers. If the Cupholder lost a challenge game, it had to relinquish the trophy. Also, if a defending champion lost its league title, the Cup would automatically go to the new league champion. A team believing itself to be worthy of a shot at hockey's ultimate prize would issue a

ENTER THE STANLEY CUP • 13

Lord Stanley announced in 1892 that Canada's champion hockey club of the moment would receive a striking silver goblet; to gain control of the trophy, another team would have to challenge and beat the reigning champion. In the more than 100 years since his bequest, there has been no greater glory for a hockey player than to drink victory champagne out of Lord Stanley's Cup.

challenge to the champion, which would then be reviewed—and either approved or rejected—by John Sweetland and Phillip Ross, two Ottawa residents. These men functioned as Stanley Cup trustees and were appointed by Lord Stanley himself before he returned home to England in 1893.

The awarding of the Stanley Cup was not always scientific. In 1894, for instance, no fewer than four of the five AHA teams finished with identical records, forcing the trustees to devise an impromptu playoff format. The final saw the Montreal AAA team beat Ottawa 3–1 in front of a then-astounding crowd of more than 5,000 fans. In 1895, the Stanley Cup champion was not even involved in the finals. This occurred when Sweetland and Ross accepted the challenge of the Queens University hockey team against the 1894 champion Montreal AAAs. Prior to that game, the Cup had been claimed by the Montreal Victorias, who finished ahead of the AAAs in the AHA standings. But the Victorias declined to defend the Cup, having already scheduled a lucra-

tive exhibition series against Ottawa in New York City, where hockey had begun to catch on. In an odd decision, the trustees announced that if Queens University won the game, they would have to beat the Victorias in order to be awarded the Stanley Cup. But if the AAAs won, the Cup would go to the Victorias. In other words, the AAA team knew going into its match with Queens that regardless of the outcome it could not win the Stanley Cup. Despite this handicap, the AAAs gained an easy 5–1 win. And the Vics were crowned Cup champions.

In 1896, the first East-West battle for the Stanley Cup was held when the Winnipeg Victorias, champions of the Manitoba Hockey League, beat the Montreal Victorias 2–0. (Many teams called themselves the Victorias during this time, as Canadians were still British subjects and Queen Victoria ruled England.) Eastern hockey fans, who figured Montreal's city slickers would teach Winnipeg's bumpkins a lesson, were shocked at the outcome. The truth was that Winnipeg had dominated the Manitoba shocked at the outcome. The truth was that Winnipeg had dominated the Manitoba Hockey League for years and in fact only a year earlier had defeated three top eastern teams during an exhibition tour of eastern Canada. The Winnipeg players were also used to playing in some of the coldest temperatures known to humans—by comparison, the weather in Montreal must have seemed almost balmy.

The game featured some notable participants. The shutout was recorded by goalie Whitey Merritt, who skated to his position wearing a pair of cricket pads. The winning goal was scored by Dan Bain, the son of a wealthy dry-goods merchant in Winnipeg. Bain was known as a tremendous all-around athlete and an unfailing gentleman. Had Lord Stanley himself handpicked the ideal young man to represent hockey, he could hardly have done better.

Hockey's First Dynasty

Victoria Rink in Montreal, the center of the fast-growing hockey world during the 1890s

The 1897 Montreal Victorias, fresh off their first championship, pose with the Stanley Cup.

The defeat at the hands of Winnipeg proved to be a mere bump in the road for the Montreal Victorias, as they were well on the way to becoming hockey's first great club. The Vics had a dominant team, with top performers at nearly every position. On defense (or *point,* as the position was called back then) were Mike Grant and Graham Drinkwater. In goal was Gord Lewis. Montreal's rover, the diminutive Russell Bowie, ranked among the finest players of his time. Bob Macdougall played center, with Ernie McLea and Cam Davidson on the wings. This formidable team traveled to Winnipeg in December 1896 on a quest to reclaim the championship.

The excitement surrounding this match shows how popular the Stanley Cup had become in just a few years. In Winnipeg, seats to the game sold for $10 or more. In Montreal, enormous crowds gathered outside telegraph offices for play-by-play accounts of the action. Winnipeg scored the first three goals, but Montreal, led by McLea's score at 5–5 and eventually they won 6–5 in sudden death.

A year later the Vics defended their hold on the Cup with a 14–2 victory over the Ottawa Capitals, champions of the Central Canada Hockey Association. The Ottawa-Montreal meeting was supposed to be a two-game series, with total goals deciding victory if the teams split their games. But after getting creamed in the opener, Ottawa canceled the second game in the "best interests of hockey." The Montreal Victorias were so good in 1898 that no one dared to issue a challenge, so they simply kept the Cup.

At a time when the sport was beginning to spread across Canada's borders into the United States—and even across the Atlantic to Europe (France, most notably) and the Scandinavian countries—Montreal was establishing itself as the center of the hockey world thanks to the dominance of the Victorias. In 1899, the Vics won the Cup again, but not without stirring up a major controversy. After scoring a 2–1 comeback win against Winnipeg in the first of a two-game series, they took a 3–2 lead in Game Two, with 8,000 fans cheering them on. With twelve minutes to play in the second half (it would be a few more years before hockey adopted the three-period format) Montreal's Bob Macdougall sent Winnipeg star Tony Gingras sprawling with a vicious slash across his knees. When referee Bill Findlay imposed a mere two-minute penalty, Dan Bain pulled his teammates off the ice in protest. Findlay, insulted by this display, went home. It took a search party to fetch him and convince him to return to the game. By the time he did, a couple of Winnipeg players had already changed into their street clothes and left the premises; those who remained were still refusing to play unless Findlay ejected Macdougall for ungentlemanly conduct. The referee told them he would not be "pushed around" and awarded the game to the home team. The Cup trustees upheld his decision, and the Victorias went into the books as Stanley Cup champions once again.

The end of the club's dominance came a few weeks later in the final game of the season. The Victorias were tied for first place in the newly formed Canadian Amateur Hockey League (CAHL) with the Montreal Shamrocks. The Shamrocks stunned the Vics 1–0 before 8,000 people to win the league championship and take the Stanley Cup away. The Shamrocks, who were also known as the Fighting Irish, were immediately challenged by Queens University but defended the Cup with a 6–2 victory. The team defended the Cup successfully two more times during 1900, defeating the Winnipeg Vics in February and the Halifax Crescents in March. The Shamrocks were led by captain Harry Trihey and featured two of the era's best players, Art Farrell and Fred Scanlon. Although they were initially viewed as upstarts, the Shamrocks were deserving champions. Unlike other teams, they actually used set passing plays and established regular skating patterns in the offensive zone. This was called a scientific approach, although these plays are executed quite easily even at the pee-wee level today.

Hockey was still quite primitive at the turn of the century, though, and forward passing was not yet legal. Most skaters simply tried to muscle their way toward the net and then smack the puck past the goalie, so the Shamrocks' drop passes and dish-offs must have seemed quite magical to fans at the turn of the century. In 1901, the

Winnipeg Victorias reappeared on the Stanley Cup scene, and they had a surprise for the Shamrocks. Dan Bain had trained his team to counter the Shamrock plays and equipped his players with new skates featuring lighter, faster tubular blades. Winnipeg scored in the final minute of the first game to win 4–3, then held Montreal to a 3–3 tie at the end of regulation in the second contest. The first official overtime in Stanley Cup history followed, with Bain netting the winner four minutes into the extra period.

Winnipeg successfully defended its title in January 1902 against the Ontario Hockey Association champion Toronto Wellingtons. But in March the Montreal AAAs took a best-of-three series against Winnipeg by shutting down Bain, Gingras, and Scanlon. This feat earned the Montreal defense the nickname Little Men of Iron. The AAAs proved their defeat of the Victorias was not a fluke when, 11 months later, they beat Winnipeg again to hold on to the Stanley Cup. Montrealers were delighted to have the trophy back where they felt it belonged. They did not suspect, however, that the center of the hockey universe was about to shift from Montreal again, this time to the nation's capital in Ottawa.

The Silver Seven

The 1903 CAHL season saw the Ottawa Hockey Club and Montreal Victorias finish with six wins apiece. This meant that the Montreal AAAs, who finished third behind them, would have to relinquish the Stanley Cup. But to whom? It was decided that the two first-place teams would play a two-game series to decide the league title and ownership of the Cup. After battling to a

1–1 tie in Montreal, they journeyed to Ottawa, where the hometown boys overwhelmed the Victorias 8–0. The Ottawa players were immediately dubbed the Silver Seven, and for the next three years they defended the Stanley Cup as vigorously as any team in history. The Silver Seven were a group of tough, fast players who could beat an opponent with their fists or their hockey skills. Typically, they used both.

The team was led by a relentless little center named Frank McGee, who doubled as a rover when the Silver Seven needed extra help on defense. Prior to joining the Ottawa Hockey Club, he had lost an eye, thus earning the predictable nickname One-Eye McGee. A fast skater and amazing stickhandler, McGee was so far advanced for his era that he routinely scored three to five goals a game. The other stars on the Silver Seven were the three Gilmour brothers—Billy, Dave, and Suddy. McGee and the Gilmours

The Ottawa Hockey Club took the Stanley Cup in 1903 and successfully defended it nine times over the next three years. The Silver Seven were fast, skilled, and always tough when it counted.

accounted for all eight goals in the 1903 shutout of the Montreal Victorias. Backing up this foursome were the team's best defenseman, Hod Stuart, and his brother, Bruce. In goal was Bouse Hutton. In all, 16 different players appeared for the club during its reign as Stanley Cup champion.

Two days after winning the Cup, the Ottawans found themselves on the ice defending their title against the Manitoba/ Northwestern Hockey League champs from Rat Portage. A tiny town in northwest Ontario, Rat Portage is still in the books as the smallest community ever to get a shot at hockey's grandest trophy. Only one player on the Thistles was of legal age, but they were a fine hockey club, with stars Si Griffis and Billy McGimsie leading the charge. McGee and the Gilmours once again accounted for every Ottawa goal as the Silver Seven disposed of this two-game challenge 6–2, 6–4, despite playing under scary conditions. Artificial ice making was still years away, so the players were at the mercy of Mother Nature. It was mid-March and the ice was beginning to melt, and even though the game was played "indoors," the arena was built around a stretch of frozen river. Ice hockey in these conditions was dangerous business; players had been known to fall through river ice and disappear forever, and though no one perished in pursuit of the Cup on this day, the puck did skitter onto a dark patch of ice and vanish at one point during the second game. There were parts of the rink that even the players did not dare explore. The victory marked the end of the 1903 season and the first of nine successful Stanley Cup defenses by the Silver Seven.

Such was the reputation of the Ottawa Silver Seven that, even after losing several key players to Doc Gibson's International Pro Hockey League, the club could attract highly talented replacements. Rat Westwick and Alfie Smith came aboard, joining McGee and Suddy Gilmour on the four-man front line, while future Hall of Famers J. B. Hutton and Harvey Pulford shored up the defense. In January 1904, Ottawa defended the Stanley Cup against the Winnipeg Rowing Club, led by Joe Hall, hockey's dirtiest player. Bad Joe, who specialized in cross-checking, butt-ending, and high-sticking, was disliked even by his own teammates. He and captain Billy Breen gave the Silver Seven all they could handle in the best-of-three series, but a shutout by Bouse Hutton sealed Ottawa's victory in the deciding match.

Shortly after this triumph, the Silver Seven had a falling out with the Canadian Amateur Hockey League and decided to play independently. The new CAHL champions, the Quebec Hockey Club, felt that it should be awarded the Stanley Cup. But the trustees were not inclined to strip Ottawa of its prize, especially after the Silver Seven bested the Toronto Marlboros of the Ontario Hockey Association, the Montreal Wanderers of the Federal Amateur Hockey League, and the Brandon Hockey Club of the Manitoba/Northwestern Hockey League— all in the span of six weeks.

The series with the Wanderers ended abruptly when Montreal refused to play unless the abysmal conditions of Ottawa's Aberdeen Pavilion were improved. After regulation, the first game was tied 5–5, but the Wanderers would not take the ice for the overtime period. After some unsuccessful negotiating the series was canceled and the Cup was awarded to Ottawa. The Brandon series was a blowout for the Silver Seven

HOCKEY GOES SOUTH OF THE BORDER

Although ice hockey had been played for decades in Canada, during the late 19th century it was virtually unknown in the United States outside the northeastern region. That began to change in the early part of the 1890s, when students at American universities began to become interested in the sport. In 1893, Yale University tennis stars Arthur Foote and Malcolm Chace happened upon a hockey game while playing some winter matches in Canada, and they were hooked. Upon their return to the Yale campus in New Haven, Connecticut, they showed the game to their classmates, and teams began forming almost immediately. Farther south, in Maryland, a Canadian student attending Johns Hopkins University, C. Shearer, formed a team on campus in 1893 and then invited a squad from his native Montreal to come play. In other schools around the country, Canadian-born students played the game whenever they could find a frozen pond, and in no time their fellow Americans joined in the fun.

In 1896, the first U.S. hockey league was formed in New York City, with four clubs participating. The following year, a league started play in Baltimore. By the turn of the century hockey had spread to grade schools, prep schools, and athletic clubs all over the United States, especially in the Midwest and Northeast. In 1902, New York City had three leagues, and amateur circuits were operating in Boston, Philadelphia, Chicago, Pittsburgh, Cleveland, and Washington, D.C. The caliber of play was far below that of the Canadian amateurs, but it was good enough to spur interest in matches and draw paying fans.

By this time professionalism had found its way into hockey, albeit in a rather unlikely form. In 1897, a hockey-playing dentist by the name of John Gibson moved

In 1897, Doc Gibson's club in Portage Lake, Michigan, became the first team to openly field a team of paid professionals. Within a few years many of Canada's top players were coming to the United States to play for pay; the top Canadians on this 1905 Portage Lake team were brothers Hod and Bruce Stuart, the last two seated players on the right.

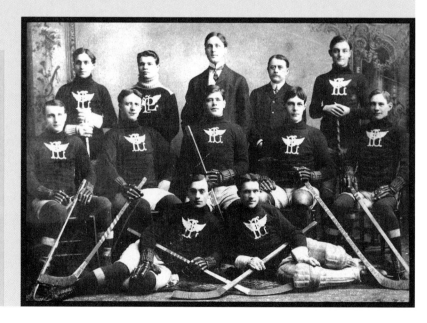

his practice from Kitchener, Ontario, to the copper mining town of Houghton, Michigan. Doc, as he was called by patients and teammates, had been receiving under-the-table payments while playing for the Berlin hockey club in Kitchener, causing the club to be expelled from the Ontario Hockey Association. After settling in Michigan, he formed the Portage Lake club and began paying top Canadians to come south and play for him. American fans, curious to see top-notch hockey, happily paid 50 cents or a dollar to watch Portage Lake teach the top amateur clubs a lesson; the team went 24–2. Gibson's team even played a few games in Canada, scoring a victory over the Montreal Wanderers, one of the best teams in all of hockey.

Although the identity of hockey's first professional player is a mystery, it is abundantly clear that playing for pay was not an American invention. The Portage Lake players returned home after the season and went right back into Canadian amateur hockey with hardly a peep from the OHA. They lost neither the respect of Canadian fans nor their amateur status. Everyone knew they had probably been receiving money under-the-table before they went to America. In fact, dozens of top Canadian players during the 1890s were known to have been compensated for their services. In 1904, however, Doc Gibson made it official. He formed the International Pro Hockey League (IPHL), marking the sport's first professional circuit. Some Canadian fans found this development quite revolting, and typically American. Leave it to the United States to take a perfectly good sport and ruin it with money.

The best Canadian players did not share this view, especially when the bidding for star players started exceeding hundreds of dollars per game. The first well-known players to head south were defensive star Hod Stuart of the Ottawa Silver Seven and Fred "Cyclone" Taylor, arguably the most exciting player in all of amateur hockey. They were followed by Sprague Cleghorn, Newsy Lalonde, Art Ross, and Spunk Sparrow, each of whom was well known throughout the hockey-playing world. A few months into the first IPHL season, the entire Sault Ste. Marie team joined the league, ending forever any thought of Canadian hockey remaining a purely amateur affair.

Although the quality of play was not quite up to Canadian standards, hockey in the United States did benefit from good old Yankee ingenuity. By 1910, the first modern indoor rink with artificial ice had been perfected. The idea was not new to the Canadians—they had been building sheltered stands around natural rinks for years as a means of charging admission and providing a small measure of comfort to hockey fans. But the American introduction made it possible to put thousands of people in the stands at a higher ticket price, generating huge revenues for a game that looked to have winter all to itself. Outside of a strange new game called basketball, ice hockey had virtually no competition for the North American sports dollar from December through March.

but nonetheless notable for the first appearance in Stanley Cup competition of a young defenseman who would play a significant role in hockey's formative years: Lester Patrick.

In January 1905, the Silver Seven found themselves defending the Stanley Cup once again. This time, the challenger was a team from Dawson City in far northwestern Canada. Though barely a speck on the map today, Dawson City was well known to Canadians in 1905. Carved out of the wilderness, Dawson City had gone from a few dozen inhabitants to a population of more than 150,000 when gold was discovered in the Yukon region. It was reputedly the roughest, toughest town in the world, especially when the gold ran out and people started getting angry and desperate. From this concentration of rabble came a tough, talented hockey team called the Klondikers. They persuaded a wealthy prospector to finance their 4,400-mile journey to Ottawa with the promise that they would keep Dawson "on the map" by bringing home the Stanley Cup. The first leg of the trip—to the Alaskan port of Skagway—was accomplished by dogsled in temperatures hitting –20°F. The Klondikers missed their boat by two hours and had to hang around the docks for five days until another boat was available to take them south to Seattle. From there, the players backtracked north by rail to Vancouver, where they finally caught a train that would take them across the continent to Ottawa.

Exhausted from their 24-day trek, the Klondikers asked to have their best-of-three series postponed a week. The Silver Seven, having just joined the Federal Amateur Hockey League, could not accommodate this wish, as it conflicted with the league schedule. The first game went to Ottawa 9–2, with the Klondikers skating sluggishly and earning many penalties for rough play. Prior to the second contest, one of the Dawson City starters was asked for his appraisal of prolific scorer Frank McGee, who had netted just one of the Silver Seven's nine goals in that first game. The player cracked that he did not look like much. This remark found its way back to the Ottawa star, and he came out blazing with four goals in the first half. Not satisfied with this effort, McGee decided to send a message in the second half. He scored 10 more goals— including a record 8 straight during one stretch—netting 4 in the span of 140 seconds.

Riding high from its blowout of the Klondikers, Ottawa underestimated the Rat Portage team that challenged for the Cup that March. This was a different club than the one the Silver Seven had beaten two years earlier. It was faster and far more skilled, as witnessed by the 9–2 beating they administered to Ottawa in the first game of their three-game series. Prior to the second game, Ottawa fans snuck onto the ice and spread salt to slow down the Thistle skaters and give the physically superior Silver Seven players a chance to throw their weight around. This resulted in a 4–2 Ottawa win. In the deciding game, McGee scored a hat trick, including the game winner in a 5–4 thriller.

Ottawa made two more successful Stanley Cup defenses in 1906 after jumping to the new Eastern Canada Amateur Hockey Association (ECAHA). Against Queens University, Alf Smith scored five times in a 16-7 win for the Silver Seven. His brother, Harry, scored five times in the second game, which also went to Ottawa,

12–7. A few weeks later, a challenge was accepted from Smiths Falls, which had succeeded Ottawa as the FAHL champion. McGee starred in this series with nine goals in two games, which the Silver Seven won 6–5 and 8–2.

The team's remarkable run finally came to an end in mid-March, when it ended the season in a flat-footed tie with the Montreal Wanderers, who had also jumped to the ECAHA. A two-game series was scheduled, with total goals deciding the league title (and therefore the Stanley Cup) should the teams split their games. The skies darkened almost immediately for the Silver Seven as the Wanderers blew them off the ice in the first game 9–1. Needing to win the second game by eight goals in order to hold on to the Cup, Ottawa put on an amazing performance and led the game 9–1 in the closing minutes. But Lester Patrick—who had become Montreal's best all-around player after coming over from the Brandon club—netted a pair of late goals to give the Wanderers a 12–10 scoring advantage over the two games and the Stanley Cup.

Ottawa's 10 consecutive Stanley Cup wins came at a time when hockey was still very much in its infancy. Yet the Silver Seven's record of dominance remains one of the great team accomplishments in the history of North American sports.

The Pros Take Over

For a growing number of amateur hockey fans, the U.S.-based IPHL was the last straw. The amateur game was losing its luster, especially when its best players routinely crossed the border to play for pay. Attendance at legitimate amateur contests dwindled while fans rushed to watch games between teams that were known to pay their top players. By 1907, there were dozens of semipro teams playing in Canada, and they began to drive the demand for top players sky-high. This had a negative impact on the IPHL, which could not afford to pay the going rate for top players and stay in business. It was not that American fans refused to pay for great hockey—on the contrary, the league sold out a high percentage of its games. The problem was that the IPHL facilities were too small. The league could have sold thousands more tickets, but it had no place to put the fans. After the 1906–7 season, the league went out of business, a victim of its own popularity.

This was an extraordinary bit of luck for Canada, which had watched in dismay for many years as its best players headed to America. Now it had them back. Almost immediately, the Ontario Professional Hockey League began play, and in 1909 the well-established Eastern Canada Amateur Hockey League dropped "Amateur" from its name and became a pro circuit.

Ambrose O'Brien, a railroad tycoon who owned the Renfrew Millionaires, wanted to join the ECHL but was refused admission. Angered by this snub, he organized a third pro league, the National Hockey Association. The NHA started with five teams, concentrated in the eastern part of Canada. Two were located in Montreal, with the Wanderers attracting an English-speaking following. O'Brien thought it would be a good idea to have a team representing the city's enormous French-speaking population, so he started a team called Les Canadiens. Almost immediately, two more teams were added, bringing the NHA's roster of first-year franchises to seven.

The NHA pioneered some important changes in hockey, the most notable of which was the reduction of team players from seven men to six. The rover position was eliminated, partly to save on salaries and partly because new defensive formations created in the OHL had shown a team did not need this player. With the number of skaters reduced by two, NHA games were faster and more exciting, and the crowds seemed to enjoy this change. The new league also went from two 30-minute periods to three 20-minute periods. This kept players fresher and created an extra intermission during which fans might purchase more food, drinks, and souvenirs. The changes paid off handsomely, as pro hockey boomed during the years prior to World War I.

On the other side of the continent, the sport was also extremely popular, but there was nothing in the way of a professional league to draw fans into arenas. This became obvious to Frank and Lester Patrick, who had played for O'Brien's Renfrew team in 1909–10 before heading west to help their father, Joe, with his lumber business in Vancouver, British Columbia. Upon their arrival in Vancouver, the Patricks started to organize the Pacific Coast Hockey Association (PCHA) and recruited top players from the East to join. Soon a steady stream of talent began flowing west. Taylor and Lalonde went, as did Frank Nighbor, and several more top performers followed. One year, Vancouver boasted seven future Hall of Famers on its roster.

The Patricks had witnessed the demise of Doc Gibson's league and vowed not to make the same mistake. They invested $300,000 from the family business in two beautiful arenas with artificial ice-making capabilites. Their crowning achievement

was the 10,500-seat building in Vancouver. When the crowds came, they would be ready. The crowds did come when the first PCHA season began in January 1912, and the Patricks were hailed as geniuses.

The Patricks were indeed gifted hockey innovators. They put numbers on uniforms so fans could keep track of which players were on the ice and came up with the idea of printing and selling programs so the fans could read all about the players. The brothers divided the playing surface into three parts with the addition of two blue lines and legalized forward passing between the two lines. This sped the game up dramatically.

The Patricks introduced the concept of league playoffs and kept detailed statistics on goals so fans could follow their favorite players in the newspapers. They also created a totally new stat, the assist, to recognize the contributions of players who set up scoring plays. In the PCHA, goalies could drop to the ice or make a kick save, which for the first time brought some glamour to this position. These moves would have drawn fines and even penalties in other leagues, which allowed only stick and glove saves. The Patricks also brought to hockey the penalty shot, which they borrowed from soccer. The only area in which they lagged behind other leagues was their insistence on sticking with seven-man teams.

Frank and Lester were pretty fair players, too. Frank, who ran the Vancouver team, was one of its top performers. Lester, who ran the Victoria franchise, was its best player. A defenseman, he liked to catch opponents napping and bring the puck up ice himself, creating a numbers advantage for his Cougars. This was a strategy many credit to players of the 1960s and 1970s,

The Victoria Cougars of the Pacific Coast Hockey Association. Sitting second from right is Lester Patrick, who with his brother Frank founded the PCHA, built a string of high-quality arenas, and rethought a number of the game's rules. Lester Patrick was also history's first attacking defenseman—he would bring the puck up ice himself when he saw it would give his team a man advantage.

but it was Lester Patrick who first saw the possibilities. He was already an experienced veteran by this time, having captained the Montreal Wanderers to the Stanley Cup in 1906. He would remain a pivotal figure in pro hockey for many decades to come.

By the 1913–14 season, the Stanley Cup competition—originally an amateurs-only affair—had opened up to all teams. The Victoria Cougars issued a challenge to the NHA to play for the Cup. Jealous and annoyed by the PCHA's brashness and success, the NHA flatly refused. But the Cup's trustees overruled the association and forced it to send its champion to meet Victoria. When Victoria won, the NHA refused to relinquish the Stanley Cup!

The Patricks relished any opportunity to antagonize the eastern hockey establishment. Later that year they expanded the PCHA into the United States, setting up shop in the hockey-mad city of Portland, Oregon. The following season, they estab-

lished a franchise in Seattle, Washington. The Patricks also pressed their claim that the PCHA league champion should automatically qualify for the Stanley Cup. This brought about the possibility of a U.S.-based club winning the Cup and taking it across the border. If fans in eastern Canada were annoyed that some of their best players would be performing in the U.S. again, they were absolutely horrified by the possibility of their sacred trophy falling into American hands. The NHA owners appealed to the Stanley Cup trustees to bar the PCHA from competing on this basis, but they saw it differently. If the Cup could be won by an American team, then that made it an international trophy. They went even further and decreed that the Cup would go to the winner of a postseason contest between the PCHA and NHA champions.

Sure enough, the Portland Rosebuds won the PCHA title in 1916 and nearly beat the Montreal Canadiens in a five-game

The humiliating Stanley Cup defeat handed the Montreal Canadiens in 1917 by the PCHA's Seattle Metropolitans—the representative of an upstart West Coast league, and a team from the *United States* no less—was the last straw in the unraveling of the National Hockey Association. The National Hockey League would take its place the next season.

series. The following season, to the utter delight of the Patricks, the Seattle Metropolitans won the PCHA title. The Mets traveled clear across the continent to play the Canadiens but upon arriving in Montreal refused to leave their train unless the NHA promised to surrender the Stanley Cup if the "unthinkable" happened and the Canadiens lost. NHA officials, insulted and embarrassed, gave their word, and the series began. Seattle took a two-games-to-one lead, then thrashed Montreal 9–1 to win the Cup. No one knew it at the time, but this was the last time an NHA team would appear on the ice.

The Birth of the NHL

After limping through the first few years of World War I, the National Hockey Association found itself in deep trouble during the early months of 1917. Only five teams remained in the league; the future did not look good. The war was continuing to siphon off manpower and fans, the public was angry about the Americans taking the Stanley Cup, and the Toronto Arenas (or Blueshirts, as they were often called) were sitting on a powder keg of a problem thanks to their stubborn owner, Eddie Livingstone. The

Frank Calder, the first commissioner of the NHL, guided the league for some 25 years.

team's star left wing, Cy Denneny, settled his family in Ottawa and asked Livingstone to trade him to the Senators so he could spend the winter with his wife and kids. When the owner refused, Denneny declined to suit up for the Arenas, and he was slapped with a two-month suspension. Denneny was a popular player around the league, and some of the NHA's other stars started talking about showing a little solidarity and coming to his aid. Perhaps forming a union would be the answer, they thought . . . or maybe just a strike would do.

Terrified at the prospect of dealing with a player's union, association president

HOCKEY AND THE GREAT WAR

As part of the British empire, Canada entered World War I in the summer of 1914. This development could not have come at a worse time for pro hockey. Many of the game's best players went to war, as did many of the young men who regularly attended PCHA, OHL, and NHA contests. Many thousands of men across Canada decided they would try to avoid military service, and police began to raid the stands at pro hockey games. This practice drove away countless fans, whether they were draft-dodgers or not, and also put a big drain on league revenues.

No one wanted the sport to die during the war, least of all the Canadian government. In fact, the army organized several hockey teams with former pros and they played exhibitions all over Canada to boost morale. One team, the Northern Fusiliers of the 228th Battalion, was so good it gained entry into the National Hockey Association. This could have been a brilliant public relations move both for the army and pro hockey. Unfortunately, it blew up in everyone's face. Apparently, the team was able to recruit the best former pros by promising them that under no circumstances would they see action in Europe. This was a great enticement when the team was formed in the fall of 1916, for casualties on the front lines were reaching appalling levels. When word of this arrangement leaked out, the NHA was heavily criticized, the 228th was shipped out to France, and the team disbanded. With only five teams left, the NHA was in trouble. When the Canadiens lost the Stanley Cup to Seattle that spring, the NHA was the laughing stock of hockey.

Frank Robinson and the other NHA owners strong-armed Livingstone into trading Denneny to Ottawa. Prior to the start of the 1917–18 season, the owners of the Montreal Canadiens, Montreal Wanderers, Quebec Bulldogs, and Ottawa Senators agreed that they wanted to get rid of Livingstone. Rather than kick him out of the NHA and endure a lengthy legal battle, they decided to leave the association en masse and form their own league without him. Thus, from the ashes of the NHA rose the NHL, the National Hockey League.

The owners asked Robinson to continue his good work as NHL commissioner, but he declined, saying he wanted no part of this skulduggery. In his place the NHL owners promoted league secretary Frank Calder. Toronto did join the league before the season got under way, but not until Livingstone had relinquished ownership of the team. Rumors persisted for years that he was still secretly running the Arenas. The readmission of the Arenas was well timed, for the Bulldogs were unable to start the season because of the previous year's heavy financial losses. Quebec's players were redistributed until the franchise reactivated itself for the 1919–20 campaign.

The NHL's first season was not a good one. In fact, it was a disaster. In January, Montreal's Westmount Arena burned down, leaving the Canadiens and Wanderers—who shared the building—without a home. The Canadiens finished the schedule at the 3,200-seat Jubilee rink, while the Wanderers just gave up and canceled the remainder of their season. With three teams left in the league, the NHL staggered home, with the Arenas winning the championship. Toronto did manage to beat Vancouver for the Stanley Cup, one of two bright spots in an

In the NHL's first season, "Phantom" Joe Malone scored 44 goals in a mere 20 games, a pace never equaled by another player. He is pictured here in the Quebec Bulldog uniform he wore as a young forward in the NHA.

otherwise depressing season. The other highlight of the NHL's inaugural campaign was the play of Joe Malone. Originally the property of the Quebec Bulldogs, he went to the Canadiens after Quebec pulled out of the league. There he scored at a clip unsurpassed to this day, netting 44 goals in just 20 games.

The NHL's second season was also a disaster, as the schedule was canceled after just 18 games. An influenza epidemic was sweeping across Canada, and people were not about to risk their lives just to see a hockey game. The Canadiens won the NHL title and traveled to Seattle to take on the Metropolitans for the Stanley Cup. At the beginning of the series, Seattle's enforcer, Joe Hall, fell ill and was hospitalized with the flu. When he died less than a week later, the series was abruptly canceled and the Stanley Cup was not awarded for the one and only time in its history.

The new league finally began to turn the corner during the 1919–20 season. A lot of good players were returning from the war, the Canadian economy was strong, and the NHL had legalized forward passing the season before. Meanwhile, the Toronto Arenas—who went from first to worst in 1918–19—changed their name to the St. Patricks and donned beautiful bright green uniforms. Another bit of good news was that the Quebec Bulldogs became an active team again. They asked for, and got, the players they had relinquished back in 1917, including Malone, who scored 38 times and tallied a record seven goals in one game. Despite the heroics of their goal-scoring star, the Bulldogs finished last in both halves of the NHL's split season, and they decided to fold the team at year's end.

The Ottawa Senators, behind the crafty net work of Clint Benedict, finished first in both halves, winning the league title outright. Benedict was hockey's first fall-down goalie. Despite the NHL's rule against hitting the ice to block shots, he pioneered this style by pretending to slip or be pushed at just the right moment. When other goalies began copying Benedict, the league loosened its restrictions and eventually wiped out the rule stating that goalies had to remain upright at all times. Behind Benedict's wonderful acting performance, the Senators went on to defeat the Seattle Metropolitans for the 1920 Stanley Cup.

The Hamilton Tigers replaced the Bulldogs for the 1920–21 campaign, giving the NHL the minimum four teams it needed. Malone put on his third uniform in three years and had another excellent season. His supporting cast was made up of former Bulldogs and a handful of youngsters sent over by the St. Patricks in a generous move to keep the league balanced. One of those players was second-year man Babe Dye, who had toiled with some distinction for Toronto the season before. In the 1920 opener he whipped two shots past the Toronto goalie in a 5–0 win for the Tigers. The St. Patricks, realizing their error, took him back after the game and sent Hamilton a backup goalie. (Generosity was one thing; stupidity was something else.) Dye scored 33 more goals to lead the NHL. During the 1920s he would establish himself as one of pro hockey's most lethal offensive players, scoring at a clip that one associates with modern players such as Wayne Gretzky and Brett Hull. The St. Pats lost to the Ottawa Senators in the NHL playoffs, but Ottawa represented the league well, taking the Stanley Cup again, this time from the

THE BIG FIVE

During the formative years of professional hockey, a special group of five players took the game to a new level. Fred Taylor, Joe Malone, Newsy Lalonde, Cy Denneny, and Georges Vezina were the sport's first superstars. Each moved hockey forward with on-ice contributions and off-ice celebrity.

Taylor was the first player whose name was known throughout Canada and who could boost attendance wherever he appeared. His long, smooth strides and ability to shift direction at full speed enabled him to cut between defenders and swoop in on goal, often without being touched. Taylor developed his highly advanced skating technique as a boy growing up in Ontario, and by the time he was 18 he had already acquired several nicknames, including Thunderbolt, Whirlwind, and Tornado. However, the handle that stuck was Cyclone, which he acquired as a member of the Ottawa Senators in the years prior to World War I. Taylor led the Senators to Stanley Cup wins five times, then defected west to the PCHA, where he joined the Vancouver Millionaires. He won the Stanley Cup with Vancouver in 1915 and was the star of the 1918 final, though his team lost to the NHL's Toronto Arenas. Taylor, who actually spent a good portion of his career as a defenseman, thrilled crowds with his end-to-end charges. He was also the first player who could skate backward at full speed. His fame was such that even American fans knew of his exploits. During the off-season Taylor and an ever-changing supporting cast would barnstorm around the U.S. and regularly sell out large arenas.

The NHL came along a year or so too late for Fred (Cyclone) Taylor, a player legendary for his skating ability—he was known to outsprint opponents down the ice while skating *backward.*

Like Taylor, Malone was also a man ahead of his time. He was playing center for the NHA's Quebec Bulldogs when the rover position was being eliminated and the game was beginning to open up. Scoring chances started to come his way in great abundance, and Malone—an excellent shooter with great accuracy and a quick release—found himself in the right place at the right time. Phantom Joe had a sixth sense for where the puck would end up after a stick save or a scramble along the boards, and before anyone could move to check him his shot was in the net. In 1913, he made headlines by scoring nine goals in the opening game of the Stanley Cup against the Sydney Miners, and he scored eight in a game against the powerful Montreal Wanderers in 1917. When the NHL began play and Quebec folded, Malone was picked up by the Montreal Canadiens. He was moved to left wing on a line with stars Newsy Lalonde and Didier Pitre, and he proceeded to set records that would never be broken. Malone scored five times in the season opener and finished the 1917–18 campaign with 44 goals in 20 games. After returning to the Bulldogs in 1919, he set a league record with seven goals in a game and finished with 39 in 24 contests. By the time defensive and goaltending strategies caught up with Malone, he was ready to retire. Ironically, while Malone played he was never a crowd favorite and never made much money from hockey. He was a quiet, workmanlike performer who was content to contribute and never played to the crowds.

His Montreal teammate Lalonde knew how to play to the fans, and he was absolutely adored. He was already one of Canada's top lacrosse players when, at the age of 20, he joined the Toronto Trolley Leaguers and led them to the 1908 Stanley Cup, which they lost to the Montreal Wanderers. It was the beginning of a hockey career that would see Lalonde win the scoring title in four different pro leagues. He was a daring skater and supreme stickhandler, making him a marked man in many of the games he played. Lalonde was roughed up almost every time he touched the puck, but he survived by fighting right back. His on-ice tangles with Bad Joe Hall were legendary. Once, Hall practically decapitated Lalonde, slashing his windpipe. Another time, after Hall carved him for 18 stitches, Lalonde returned to the ice and broke Hall's collarbone. Years later, as teammates in Montreal, they became great friends. Though somewhat past his prime, he was a great scorer for the Canadiens in the early years of the NHL, using a quick first step to power past defenders. The likable Lalonde remained a supreme playmaker into his late thirties; he was also voted the greatest lacrosse player of the first half of the twentieth century.

Denneny also brought a special scoring touch to the ice. He too came along at a time when the game was opening up, and like Malone and Lalonde he was deadly accurate from close range. Denneny began his pro career with the Toronto Arenas in 1914 before becoming embroiled in a struggle with owner Eddie Livingstone that would eventually bring on the formation of the National Hockey League. Denneny, a left

Georges Vezina's unflappable cool in the crease earned him the nickname the Chicoutimi Cucumber. (He hailed from Chicoutimi, Quebec.) By far the best goalie in pro hockey's formative years, he set a standard of excellence for all who have followed; the award given annually to the NHL's top goalie bears his name.

wing, came into his own after joining the Ottawa Senators. Teaming with Frank Nighbor, he averaged better than a goal a game in 11 seasons with Ottawa and led the franchise to four Stanley Cups during the 1920s. A tough competitor who hated to miss even a single game, Denneny won his first scoring title at 32, despite falling down a well late in the 1923–24 season. His final season was 1928–29, when he was player-coach of the Boston Bruins and led that franchise to its first NHL championship.

The supreme netminder of these early years was Georges Vezina, whose reputation for coolness in the crease made him a hockey legend. He was by far the best of the stand-up goalies at a time when the rules forbade flopping to the ice. Vezina won the Montreal goalie job in 1910 after shutting out the Canadiens during an exhibition game against his hometown amateur club. Over the next 15 years, he led Montreal to two NHA titles and two Stanley Cups. The key to his composure probably had to do with his home life. With 22 children, Vezina probably found the prospect of stopping 50 or 60 shots relaxing compared to what he had to face when he walked through his own front door. He left the game at the age of 39, cut down by tuberculosis, but an enduring legacy remains in the award that now bears his name. Each season, the NHL's top goaltender receives the Vezina Trophy.

PCHA Vancouver Millionaires. Jack Darragh, who in 1920 had registered a hat trick in Game Five to give the Senators the Cup, came through again in 1921. He scored both goals in Game Five to seal a 2–1 Ottawa victory.

West Coast Hockey Falters

Although the PCHA was losing its grip on the Stanley Cup, its hold over western hockey fans was never more profound. The 1921 Cup opener saw 11,000 people jam into the Vancouver arena; the five-game series drew a total of 51,000. Given the level of interest out west, it was only natural that a rival pro league would form. In 1921–22, the Western Canada Hockey League (WCHL) began play, with teams in Calgary, Edmonton, Regina, and Saskatoon.

The Stanley Cup trustees agreed that the 1922 championship would be contested between the NHL winner and the victor in a playoff between the PCHA and WCHL champions. The NHL, which had voted to drop its split-season format, decided its top two finishers would meet in a postseason championship series. The first-place Toronto St. Patricks prevailed in this competition, earning the right to face Vancouver, which beat the WCHL champ Regina Capitals. The Vancouver-Toronto series was a thrilling seesaw affair that showcased the talents of Jack Adams—who had been obtained by Vancouver from Toronto that fall—and Dye, who netted 9 of the St. Patricks' 16 goals. The backbreaker was Dye's Game Five "mystery goal," a shot so hard the Vancouver goalie never saw the puck until spectators behind the goal told him to look in the net.

The balance of power in pro hockey shifted even more toward the East in the mid-1920s, as the Ottawa Senators and Montreal Canadiens won the Stanley Cup in 1923 and 1924, respectively. Prior to the 1924–25 season, the PCHA folded. Ironically, it was not for lack of fans. When hockey was being played in the magnificent PCHA arenas, the stands were packed. But during the rest of the year there was no other way to keep the buildings filled. Maintenance costs were killing the Patricks and their business partners, so they decided to kill the PCHA. The Victoria Cougars jumped to the WCHL and won that league's title in 1925 and 1926. They defeated the Canadiens for the Stanley Cup in 1925 but fell in 1926 to the Montreal Maroons when Clint Benedict shut them out three times. After the 1925–26 season, the WCHL also folded, unable to afford the big salaries that went with putting top-level pro hockey on the ice.

America Takes to Hockey

While Canada's various professional hockey leagues had been struggling for supremacy in the years before and after World War I, amateur hockey had been flourishing at the high school, college, and semipro levels in the United States. Although the skills of U.S. players hardly approached those of

their Canadian counterparts, games staged in major city arenas and armories often drew thousands. Hockey, in fact, was a more popular winter sport than basketball, which was struggling mightily to attract fans to big arenas.

New England's college-prep boarding schools were one of the major hotbeds of hockey in the United States. Temperatures in the region got cold enough to create ice for at least 10 weeks a year, and when natural ice was unavailable these private schools had the financial capacity to rent time at indoor rinks. Some schools were good enough to beat college and semipro teams, and because their alumni usually went on to become successful businessmen, large and well-heeled crowds could be expected to attend their games in cities such as Boston, New York, and Philadelphia. The same was true for college teams. Their graduates were enthusiastic supporters of all sports teams, and college hockey games provided an excellent way to socialize with fellow alumni.

America's hockey may have been of low quality, but the country was definitely developing a high-powered hockey culture all its own. The man who gave this phenomenon its initial spark was Hobey Baker, who became an American sports legend during the years prior to World War I. Baker was a startlingly gifted natural athlete. After only a few hours of observation and practice, he was able to pick up any sport he tried. Born in a posh Philadelphia suburb in 1892, he attended the St. Paul's School in Concord, New Hampshire, from age 11 until he was 18. During his years at St. Paul's, Baker developed into the finest hockey player in the U.S. He obtained special permission from the school's headmaster to skate at night;

working out on the ice of a nearby pond in near-total darkness taught him to handle the puck by feel, without looking at it. Adding to his prowess was that his St. Paul's teammates were almost as good as he was. While Baker was on the team, it regularly defeated college squads and even shut

Princeton University star Hobey Baker played hockey as no American before him had, sparking new interest in the game in the United States.

out a Princeton team that would go on later that year to win the intercollegiate hockey championship.

Baker ended up attending Princeton, where he became captain of the football team. He also played rover on the hockey team and became a star like no college hockey player before him. Baker was three strides faster than anyone else, and he could change speed and direction seemingly without effort. His ability to weave through defenders without losing his balance or the puck brought crowds roaring to their feet, and in no time at all Princeton was playing games to packed arenas in New York City. Never before had a college hockey player dominated the sports pages the way Baker did, and to this day no American-born player has ever possessed his drawing power.

After graduating from Princeton in 1914, Baker entered the business world and played hockey for the top-notch amateur St. Nick's club in New York City. Although the Canadian players who saw him grudgingly admitted he would be a star in the pros, the thought never crossed his mind. Hockey, in Baker's view, was a game to be played for love, not money. After America entered World War I, he earned a reputation as his country's best fighter pilot. He died the day the war ended, when his plane suffered a mechanical failure on a routine flight. To this day, the top college hockey player in the United States is given the Hobey Baker Award.

By the mid-1920s, hockey was firmly established as the predominant winter spectator sport in the U.S., especially in the big cities. This was of great interest to the National Hockey League, which desperately needed money. Although NHL attendance was growing steadily, the league lacked the kind of modern arenas that would ensure its continued growth. To build these hockey palaces, a huge infusion of capital was required, and the only place it was going to come from was south of the Canadian border. The decision was made to expand into the U.S. In 1924, the NHL admitted the Boston Bruins. A year later, a franchise was awarded to Pittsburgh, and the struggling Hamilton Tigers were purchased for $75,000 and moved to New York, where they were rechristened the Americans.

In 1926, three more U.S. teams joined the NHL. When the Patricks folded the PCHA, they sold the rights to their players to the NHL for a quarter of a million dollars, but in a separate deal they also sold the Portland Rosebuds and its players to investors in Chicago, who renamed them the Blackhawks. The Victoria Cougars were sold to businessmen in Detroit, who would later call their team the Red Wings. Also entering the NHL in 1926 were the New York Rangers. Including the Montreal Maroons—who were added in 1924 to attract the city's English-speaking population—the NHL numbered 10 teams in 1926–27, with more than half in the United States. It was a stunning transformation.

The NHL Comes of Age

During the late 1920s and right up until the Second World War, pro hockey evolved into a highly popular spectator sport on both sides of the border. Two of the most successful teams in the NHL during this period were the Toronto Maple Leafs and the New York Rangers. The Maple Leafs came to be in 1927, when Conn Smythe—one of ama-

teur hockey's most renowned figures—became one of the owners of the Toronto St. Patricks. A patriot through and through, he pushed to change the team's name to reflect Canada's national symbol, the maple leaf. He no doubt believed, too, that this would attract a much broader fan base.

The ever-colorful Conn Smythe put together seven Stanley Cup champion teams in his three decades as general manager of the Toronto Maple Leafs.

With Smythe functioning as club president and general manager, Toronto reversed a years-long pattern of losing and by the 1930s—with Dick Irvin behind the bench—became a perennial Stanley Cup contender. Smythe's eye for young talent resulted in the signing of three top teenagers during the 1920s: Joe Primeau, Busher Jackson, and Charlie Conacher. They spent seven seasons together as hockey's famous Kid Line. To lend leadership to the team, he swung a deal with the struggling Ottawa Senators for veteran King Clancy, who teamed with Hap Day to form the league's most formidable defensive tandem. Conacher, at right wing, was Toronto's scoring star, leading the NHL in goals five times. He was a slick puckhandler who possessed a tremendous shot, and regularly topped the 30-goal mark back when the season was less than 50 games long. Jackson played left wing, where he

Only 5′9″ tall, Frank "King" Clancy made up for his lack of size with speed, agility, and toughness. He was among the NHL's greatest attacking defensemen and most popular players.

functioned both as a goal scorer and play-maker. He won the NHL scoring title in 1932–33 and was a top player until 1939, when a shoulder injury limited his effectiveness. Primeau was one of the few clean players of his day, so much so that everyone called him Gentleman Joe. But there was nothing gentlemanly about the tenacity with which he separated an enemy skater from the puck—or how he led the Toronto attack, bearing down on defenses and then flicking the puck to his talented wingers.

From 1931–32 to 1937–38, the Maple Leafs finished first in the NHL's Canadian Division four times. But it was as a playoff team that they truly distinguished themselves, making the Stanley Cup Finals an incredible seven times in nine years from 1931–32 to 1939–40. The only knock on this team was that they had trouble nailing down that final victory. After winning it all in 1932, the Leafs fell short in the finals six times in a row. In 1933, and again in 1940, the team that did in the Leafs was the New York Rangers.

After joining the NHL in 1926–27, the Rangers won the American Division title and barely missed a trip to the Stanley Cup Finals. The next year they did make it, only to lose their home-ice advantage to the circus, which had already been scheduled to move into Madison Square Garden. Team owner Tex Rickard dealt his Rangers a huge blow by allowing the best-of-five finals to be played on the home ice of their opponents, the Montreal Maroons. No one suspected that the stage had been set for one of hockey's most famous moments. With an enemy crowd screaming at them from the standing-room-only Montreal Forum, the Rangers seemed to have no chance. After dropping Game One, their situation worsened in Game Two when goalie Lorne Chabot was lost for the series with an eye injury. Into the nets stepped white-haired coach Lester Patrick, 45 years old and not exactly in game shape. Mustering what was left of his strength and using every trick he had learned as a defender, he survived a barrage of Montreal shots to give his team a 2–1 overtime win. Not wishing to tempt fate, Patrick signed young Joe Miller as his goalie for the rest of the series. The rookie responded with two big games as the Rangers pulled out the best-of-five series for a Stanley Cup win in just their second year of existence.

The Rangers reached the Cup Finals five more times over the next 12 years, winning it all again in 1933 and 1940. During the early part of that run, New York depended on the talents of defenseman Ivan "Ching" Johnson, wingmen Bill and Bun Cook, and center Frank Boucher. All four stars came from the PCHA, so coach Patrick already knew what kind of material he had to work with. Johnson, who was already 28 when the Rangers picked him up in 1926, played another 11 seasons with New York. He was a classic battler, refusing to let an opposing puckhandler past him. He would check, clutch, grab, hack, and otherwise impede the progress of all who dared to challenge him. For this he was known as the Great Wall of China. For his skill at tying up opponents in the crease, Johnson was also called the Holding Corporation.

The Cook brothers came to New York from the Western League's Saskatoon Sheiks, with Bill playing right wing and Bun setting up shop on the opposite side of the rink. Bun was good for 15–20 goals a season, and the same number of assists.

Bill, the better of the two, led all players with 33 goals in his first NHL season and led the league in points in 1932–33. The Ranger captain was the dominant power forward of the 1920s and 1930s, blending highly developed offensive skills with a reputation as a mean fighter. Long before he tried his hand at pro hockey, Bill Cook had distinguished himself as an artilleryman during World War I. After the armistice, his hunger for action found him in the Royal Russian Army, serving as a scout against the Bolsheviks in what was ultimately a losing cause.

Centering for these two was Boucher. He had played for Patrick in Vancouver and was already a veteran at 26 when he joined the Rangers. He was a slick, stylish setup man who played hard and clean. During Boucher's eight-year NHL career, he won the Lady Byng Trophy for sportsmanlike play seven times and was eventually given the original trophy. He was also a great innovator, developing several plays around the drop pass that made it New York's most lethal weapon. Upon his retirement, the Rangers appointed him coach, and he led the team to the 1940 Stanley Cup—the last it would win for more than 50 years. As New York coach, he developed the rectangle formation for killing penalties, which is still used today, and came up with the strategy of replacing his goalie with an extra skater when trailing by a goal in the final moments of a game. The team Boucher led to the championship was nowhere near as talented as the one for which he starred—a great tribute to his work behind the bench.

Although no franchise could be said to have dominated the NHL during the years following the league's expansion into the United States, the Boston Bruins might

When New York's goalie went down to injury in Game 2 of the 1928 Stanley Cup Finals, the team's 45-year-old coach, Lester Patrick, decided to man the crease himself. The once-great defenseman played brilliantly, and when the Rangers prevailed 2–1 in overtime his teammates carried him off the ice in triumph.

have had the best team during this era. Between 1926 and 1941, they recorded 10 first-place finishes and won three Stanley Cups. When the rules on passing were relaxed in the late 1920s, the Bruins developed an offense to take advantage of these changes. The original team was assembled in the mid-1920s from amateurs and a handful of pros picked up from the folding leagues out west, including veteran forward Spunk Sparrow and defenseman Eddie Shore. Sprague Cleghorn was acquired from the Canadiens to toughen up the defense. After finishing dead last their first year, the Bruins began to improve, and within two seasons they made it to the Stanley Cup Finals. Several of the unknown amateurs plucked out of Canada by General Manager Art Ross turned into fine players, including goalie Charles Stewart and forwards Jimmy Herberts and Carson Cooper, who became an awesome scoring duo.

The player who pulled them all together, however, was Shore. He was a spectacular player in the truest sense of the word. Nothing he did was done with the least bit of subtlety. When Shore checked an opponent, he did it by hurling his body through the air. When he carried the puck up the ice—a rare move for a defenseman in the 1930s—he was either going to bull his way to the goal or get into a fight trying. Boston fans adored him, and thanks to Shore they came to see the Bruins in droves. Opposing fans hissed and booed him—but they paid their way in to see him, too. His reputation for toughness was matched by his courage and commitment, and even those who hated him had to admire his unique position in the game. Shore was voted NHL MVP four times, but he paid a huge price for this notoriety. Everyone in the league knew that the way to beat Boston was to beat up Shore. When he hung up his skates in 1941, he had broken his nose 14 times, shattered his jaw 5 times, and lost virtually all his teeth. By Shore's own count, he received 973 stitches during his career.

No player has ever given more of himself to hockey than tough-as-nails defenseman Eddie Shore of the Boston Bruins. Shore anchored the Bruin defense for 14 years and endured 5 broken jaws, 14 broken noses, and 973 stitches.

The Bruins won the Stanley Cup in 1929 and finished atop the NHL's American Division four straight times between 1928 and 1931. During these years the team featured a line called the Dynamite Trio, which consisted of right wing Dit Clapper, center Cooney Weiland, and left winger Dutch Gainor. Clapper, a large man who often used his size to break up the fights Shore started, was the first man to have a 20-year NHL career, playing his first 10 years as a

wing and his last 10 as a defenseman. His hallmark was perfection. He rarely made a mistake, either physically or mentally, and he even looked good when he played. Indeed, the only way to get Clapper really mad was to muss up his perfectly parted hair. So cherished a player was he that he was elected to the Hall of Fame while still active. Weiland, a devilishly good stickhandler who was typically good for 15 to 20 goals, went wild in 1929–30 and tallied 43 in 44 games to lead the Bruins back to the Cup Finals.

Throughout the 1930s, the Bruins remained competitive, thanks to Shore, Clapper, goalie Tiny Thompson, and the ability of Ross to keep coming up with hot young players. The Bruins returned to the finals in 1939 with a fast-paced attack featuring the famous Kraut Line of Bob Bauer, Milt Schmidt, and Woody Dumart and the stingy goaltending of rookie Frank Brimsek. In 1940, the Kraut Line finished 1-2-3 in the league in scoring, and in 1941 they produced another Stanley Cup. Schmidt, who centered the line, was the key figure for the Bruins by this time. The young star would glide up the ice, surveying the defense without ever looking down at the puck, then squeeze off the game's most feared wrist shot. Brimsek, whose nickname was Mr. Zero, took care of business on the defensive end. He recorded six shutouts in his first eight NHL games and established himself as the top goalie of the prewar years. Brimsek was also the NHL's first American-born superstar, which put his name on the sports pages from coast to coast whenever he recorded one of his 40 career shutouts.

Among the other top stars during this period was Aurel Joliat of the Montreal

Boston's Kraut Line of the late 1930s and early 1940s in action: With Bob Bauer (17) in the post and Woody Dumart (14) at the point, Milt Schmidt (15) flies toward the crease on his way to a goal.

Canadiens. Joliat, a left wing who stood 5′6″ and weighed around 140 pounds, was brought to Montreal in 1922 to replace the popular Newsy Lalonde, who had been dealt to the West Coast. Joliat made fans forget about Lalonde almost immediately, becoming a fan favorite in Montreal for the next 16 years. A lightning-quick skater with the most lethal backhand ever seen up to that time, Joliat was the kind of slippery player opponents could not afford to leave unchecked, yet often had a hard time locating. He was also a celebrated eccentric, playing with a black baseball cap that he would stop and pick up if it flew off—even in the middle of a play.

In 1923, Joliat was joined on the Canadiens by an equally beloved player, center

Howie Morenz, who became the "Babe Ruth of Canada." Happy-go-lucky and immensely talented, he captured the public's imagination in that special way that only a rare athlete can. Morenz was fast and fiery, and although he weighed in at just 165 pounds, he checked like a 200-pounder. His shot was hard and accurate, and he was even faster down the ice than Joliat. Off the ice, he was Montreal's ultimate man about town, changing suits two and three times a day and turning up in all the right places with all the right people. He and Joliat teamed up to bring the Stanley Cup to Montreal in 1924 and also led the team to back-to-back Stanley Cups in 1930 and 1931. In 1934, Montreal did the unthinkable and traded Morenz to the Blackhawks, but he returned to the team two years later. In 1937, he broke his left leg and ankle during a game against Chicago. While recovering from these injuries, Morenz suffered an embolism and died in a Montreal hospital. His casket was placed in the Montreal Forum, and tens of thousands of fans came to pay their respects.

Howie Morenz, the premier player on the Canadiens teams of the 1920s and 1930s. He is pictured here before a 1934 benefit game matching a team of NHL All-Stars against the Maple Leafs, staged to pay the medical bills of Toronto winger Ace Bailey in the aftermath of a near-fatal run-in with Eddie Shore. It was the league's first All-Star contest.

The latter half of the 1930s saw most teams struggling to make ends meet, as the Great Depression hit fans hard in the pocketbook. There was, however, a silver lining to this dark cloud. No club dominated the NHL during this period, which kept interest high in most of the league's cities. The fast-improving Detroit Red Wings won a pair of Stanley Cups in 1936 and 1937, and the Chicago Blackhawks followed their surprising 1934 Cup win with an even more shocking championship in 1938, when the team won just 14 regular season games. The New York Americans, though rarely within sniffing distance of first place, did produce the league's top scorer—left wing Sweeney Schriner averaged nearly a point a game from 1935 to 1939. Sadly, there were some teams that just could not make it. The depression claimed the Philadelphia Quakers in 1931, the Ottawa Bulldogs became the St. Louis Eagles in 1934 and folded a season later, and the Montreal Maroons called it quits following the 1937–38 campaign. The Americans transferred to Brooklyn in search of new fans in 1941, then folded at the end of the season. The team's manager, Red Dutton, became NHL president when Frank Calder died during the 1942–43 campaign. Calder had guided the NHL through turbulent times, and his passing was untimely to say the least. With the world at war, pro hockey's future was anything but clear.

Powers of the 1940s

Whereas World War II dealt a devastating blow to professional sports like football, baseball, and basketball, it was much kinder to professional hockey. Although the NHL lost many of its top players, the league pared itself down to six teams, so the trickle of talent coming into the pros was enough to keep the level of play quite high. Some historians call the 1940s hockey's Golden Age, and fans of the Red Wings, Canadiens, or Maple Leafs might be inclined to agree. These three franchises dominated hockey for more than a dozen years during and after the war, producing some of the finest teams ever to take the ice. Detroit and Montreal had the glamorous players, while Toronto had a knack for turning it on during the playoffs. The Bruins, who seemed on the verge of building a dynasty in 1941, faded out of the picture when their fabled Kraut Line enlisted in the Royal Canadian Air Force. With Canada at war with Germany, it seemed like the patriotic thing to do.

The Maple Leafs had been a consistently competitive team for a long time, but they had not won a Stanley Cup since 1932. When the war began, their prospects of winning again seemingly dimmed when 56-year-old Conn Smythe enlisted in the Canadian army to take command of an artillery unit. But Smythe had planned for his own departure by promoting his favorite defenseman, Hap Day, to coach. He also negotiated preseason deals to acquire a group of important role players, including Lorne Carr and Sweeney Schriner from the New York Americans, who would drop out of the league a year later. As Smythe saw it, the key to Toronto's success would be its depth. And he was right. In 1941–42, the Leafs dressed no fewer than nine players who reached double digits in goals—the first time that had ever happened—and won the Stanley Cup in dramatic fashion, coming back from a 3–0 deficit against the Detroit Red Wings.

Over the next few seasons, the veterans became cagey old-timers, the rookies matured, and the role players got even better. The Leafs' goaltending star, Turk Broda, was lost to the service, but in 1944–45 the team found a replacement in rookie Frank "Ulcers" McCool. McCool won the Calder Trophy as the NHL's top newcomer, then performed magnificently against the Canadiens in Toronto's upset of Montreal in the 1945 Stanley Cup semifinals. This set up a rematch with the Red Wings in the Cup Finals. Oddsmakers gave Detroit a slight edge in the series, figuring McCool could not stay hot. They were wrong: He kept the Red Wings scoreless for the first 188 minutes of the series, registering three straight shutouts. Detroit made a nice comeback to knot the series at 3–3, but Toronto ultimately prevailed.

The 1945 championship turned out to be a last gasp for this group of Maple Leafs,

Toronto center Syl Apps flips a backhand shot toward the Boston net, but goalie Frank Brimsek has a bead on it. Mr. Zero backstopped the Bruins to two Cups and won a pair of Vezina Trophies.

SYL APPS AND THE GREAT COMEBACK

The Toronto Maple Leafs were led by Syl Apps during the war years. One of the greatest all-around centers in history, Apps was Canada's version of an All-American hero. A track-and-field star in the 1936 Olympics, he did not drink or smoke, and he played hockey as cleanly as he lived, logging a mere 56 minutes in the penalty box during his career. At a time when NHL broadcasts were finally reaching all corners of Canada, Apps was his country's most admired star. He was a strong skater, an excellent passer and stickhandler, and the kind of dependable and inspiring leader a team needs when its back is against the wall. And that is exactly what happened during the 1942 Stanley Cup Finals.

The Detroit Red Wings took the first three games of the series by exploiting Toronto's lone weakness: slow-skating defenders. Detroit coach Jack Adams devised a strategy that is still in use today: He instructed his players to dump the puck into the Toronto zone as soon as they crossed center ice, then to beat the Maple Leafs to the puck along the boards. Desperate for a solution, Hap Day contacted Conn Smythe, who suggested he bench his veteran backliners and insert a couple of fresh-legged rookies. Day took Smythe's advice and further shook up the Toronto lineup by giving Apps two new linemates. He also used 18-year-old rookie Gaye Stewart (who was still in high school) in key spots when his veterans needed a rest. As he watched his team struggle for survival, Day scribbled ideas on a pad and then reviewed his notes between periods. Every time the Leafs returned to the ice, he tried something different. After a while the Red Wings did not know what to expect, and before they could respond the series was tied at 3–3.

Prior to Game Seven, Smythe arrived in Toronto to deliver one of his patented pregame speeches. To his shock, Ed Bickle, director of Maple Leaf Gardens, tried to keep him out. After Coach Day threatened to separate Bickle from his senses, Smythe was allowed into the dressing room, where he urged his former players on. After two periods, however, the Leafs had not scored. Smythe returned to the locker room prior to the final period and talked to veterans Schriner and Carr. He pointed out that the game had disintegrated into the kind of grinding, sluggish affair that would give them a chance to score if they could strike quickly. When the Red Wings drew a penalty, Day held back Apps and sent in Schriner's line. They responded with a scrappy goal to tie the score at 1–1. The Toronto role players then took over and scored the go-ahead goal, and Schriner finished off Detroit with his second goal of the night. Toronto's Cup win is still considered the greatest comeback in Stanley Cup history.

but with Smythe back from the army the team retooled quickly. Toronto added three important rookie defensemen with high-spirited Bill Barilko and college stars Jim Thompson and Gus Morton, whom Maple Leaf fans would call the Gold Dust Twins. Another newcomer, right wing Howie Meeker, won the Calder Trophy, and Smythe added hip-checking specialist Bill Ezinicki and Harry Watson to the line centered by Apps. Meanwhile, center Teeder Kennedy had come into his own as a tough, hardworking team leader with a knack for scoring big goals. Also returning from the war were a core group of veterans, including Gus Bodnar, Vic Lynn, hard-shooting Bud Poile, and Don and Nick Metz, who had played key roles in the 1942 playoffs. Finally, with Turk Broda back in the nets, the Leafs were looking formidable.

Smythe himself did not realize how formidable his team was until the 1947 playoffs rolled around. The Leafs whipped Detroit to reach a final-round series against Montreal but dropped the opener to the Canadiens 6–0. After the blowout, Montreal goalie Bill Durnan wondered aloud how Toronto even made the playoffs. He got his answer when the Maple Leafs burned him for four power-play goals in Game Two, then took three of the next four contests to win the Stanley Cup. Never before had a team so young won the NHL championship, so of course the experts predicted Toronto would mature into a perennial Cup winner.

This time, the experts were right. But Smythe was not a man to stand pat. Early in the season he engineered a monstrous trade with the Blackhawks, sending five players from his Stanley Cup team to Chicago in exchange for veteran star Max Bentley. Smythe believed that the key to winning in

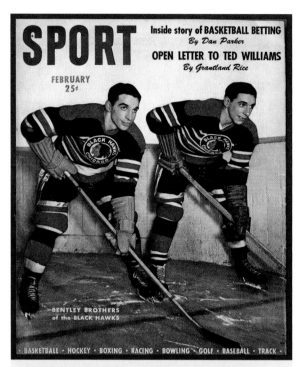

Brothers Doug and Max Bentley (right) anchored Chicago's high-powered Pony Line through most of the 1940s, winning three scoring titles between them. Max, the faster skater and slicker stickhandler of the two, joined the Maple Leafs in 1947–48 and helped them to win three Stanley Cups.

the playoffs was having fast, smart players at center. Now the Leafs had Apps, Kennedy, and Bentley, who was the league's craftiest stickhandler. The slightly built 27-year-old was the Wayne Gretzky of his era, looping around, behind, and through opponents until he had the full attention of at least two or three defenders. Then he would slip a slick little pass to an open teammate for a clear shot on goal. In Chicago, Bentley had been a setup man for high-scoring Bill Mosienko. In Toronto, he was surrounded by the deepest squad in the NHL.

The Maple Leafs easily beat Detroit in the Stanley Cup Finals to take the 1948 crown. In 1948–49, the experts who had applauded the Maple Leafs were suddenly picking against them. The odds seemed too steep for a "three-peat." Syl Apps had called it quits, and no team had ever won three NHL titles in a row. Smythe set out to make another big trade to acquire a replacement for his departed star and landed young Cal Gardner of the Rangers. As usual, the Leafs bumped along during the regular season and barely made it into the playoffs with a sub-.500 record. But once the second season

began, they were their old selves again, wiping out the Bruins in the semifinals and again beating the Red Wings in the finals behind the stellar net play of Broda, who by this time was being hailed as the best big-game goalie in all of hockey. As if Smythe himself had written the script, the goals that sealed Detroit's doom were scored by his two plum acquisitions, Gardner and Bentley.

The glamour franchise for most of the 1940s was the Montreal Canadiens. After some lean years in the late 1930s and early 1940s, the team built a good nucleus of

THE ALL-STAR GAME

The first NHL All-Star Game was played in Maple Leaf Gardens in 1947, but it was hardly a new idea. Three games had taken place before World War II as special benefits, and they proved popular enough to warrant a regular contest as soon as the league returned to normal following the war. In 1934, Toronto winger Ace Bailey was badly injured when Eddie Shore hit him from behind, and a game was held to raise money for his medical bills. In this contest, the Maple Leafs took on a team of NHL All-Stars. Three years later, a game pitting a combined team of Montreal Canadiens and Maroons against the NHL All-Stars was held to benefit the family of Howie Morenz. In 1939, the Canadiens played the All-Stars to raise money for the family of Babe Siebert, who had drowned the previous summer.

The 1947 contest pitted the defending Stanley Cup champion Maple Leafs against the NHL All-Stars; over the next three decades this format was used with great success. In 1951 and 1952, the first-team All-Stars played the second-team All-Stars, but the league reverted back to the old format. The games were played before the start of each season until the league expanded in 1966, and since then it has been a midseason event, usually between the east and the west. In 1979, the game was canceled so that a group of NHL stars could play a Soviet team, and in 1987 this format was adopted again. In 1998, the NHL created two teams—North America and The World—and played a game that underscored the tremendous talent pool from European countries such as Russia, Sweden, Finland, and the Czech Republic.

players, including left wing Toe Blake and center Elmer Lach. Blake had been playing in Montreal for years and was considered the NHL's best offensive player in the late 1930s. Lach, a swift and courageous playmaker, joined the team in 1940. Defensemen Glen Harmon, Kenny Reardon, and Butch Bouchard, who learned his hockey in Montreal from junior coaching legend Paul Stuart, also helped the Canadiens scratch their way back into contention.

A couple of years later, Stuart turned out another top player in fiery young Maurice "Rocket" Richard. Richard joined the Canadiens in 1942–43 but broke his ankle after just 16 games. The following fall, Coach Dick Irvin placed Richard alongside Lach and Blake, and with 32 goals in 46 games played, he proved to be the final piece of Montreal's puzzle. The Canadiens took off, losing only five times and finishing in first place by a whopping 25 points. Richard, Blake, and Lach were nicknamed the Punch Line, and in the 1944 playoffs they delivered knockout blows to the Maple Leafs and Blackhawks, winning the Stanley Cup in nine games. In his Stanley Cup debut, the 22-year-old Richard took charge, scoring 10 of his team's 16 goals against Chicago and either scoring or assisting on all five scores in the 5–4 overtime victory that gave Montreal the championship.

A great team needs a great goalie, of course, and the Canadiens most definitely had one in Bill Durnan. One of the best athletes ever to play pro hockey, Durnan was a famous schoolboy pitcher and goaltender. He hurled his baseball team to four provincial titles and was so dominant in the nets that one season he did not allow a single goal. In 1934, he hurt his knee roughhousing with a friend, and his hockey career

Two of history's greatest netminders, Montreal's Bill Durnan (left) and Toronto's Turk Broda, smile and shake hands after doing battle. At the close of every NHL game the combatants line up, dismiss any hard checks, high sticks, or fights that might have occurred, and shake hands as they skate past each other.

seemed over. But in 1943, at the age of 28, the Canadiens—strapped for talent during the war—took a chance and signed him off a semipro team. It turned out to be a brilliant move. During his years on the fringes of hockey, the ambidextrous Durnan had perfected the art of switching his stick from one hand to the other depending on which side a play was developing. This freed him to use his glove to cover the best shooting angles. No self-respecting pro coach would have allowed such nonsense, but because

THE ROCKET

The product of a rough neighborhood in depression-era Montreal, Maurice Richard was hungry and angry and strong. And he knew no fear. These attributes, combined with great hockey skills and an awesome physique, made Richard the most feared one-on-one competitor the game has ever known. There was nothing fancy about his game. He either went around you, through you, or over you. Richard would collect a loose puck, determine the quickest way to get to the goal, and then power up the ice like a locomotive. At times he could not be stopped. Even when defensemen willingly took penalties by wrapping themselves around his body, Richard often carried them 20 or 30 feet and still got off a shot. Richard was a goalie's nightmare. His first couple of steps were faster and more powerful than anyone else's, and he was strong enough to manhandle a defender with one arm while maintaining control of the puck with the other. Though he shot left-handed, Richard played right wing, which meant he might swoop into the middle at any time and fire a quick, accurate wrist shot. He kept everything low, especially late in games, when he knew the old-time goalie pads would be soaked and heavy with sweat and melted ice. In just his second full NHL season, Richard did something that at the time was considered impossible—he scored 50 goals in 50 games.

Fierce, fast, and powerful, Maurice (Rocket) Richard had an unequaled killer instinct around the goal; given the slightest opportunity, he could be counted on to put the puck in the net. Richard was the first player to pot 500 goals over a career.

Durnan was not in organized hockey, he was allowed to do whatever he pleased. When he arrived in Montreal, he came with two specially constructed gloves that allowed him to catch or hold a stick as he saw fit. Durnan played with the Canadiens for seven seasons and won the Vezina Trophy as the league's top goalie an incredible six times. Behind his great goaltending and the powerful Punch Line, the Canadiens finished first during the regular season each year from 1943–44 to 1946–47 and won the Stanley Cup again in 1946.

Although the Detroit Red Wings had trouble dealing with the Maple Leafs, they held their own against the rest of the league during the 1940s. In 1942–43, Jack Adams's team finished in first place and won the Stanley Cup after reaching the finals the previous two years. Aside from the team's three excellent left wingers—Sid Abel, Don Grosso, and Carl Liscombe—and center Syd Howe, the Wings weren't exactly blessed with high-quality talent. Still, with Adams behind the bench, the Wings were always competitive and fashioned a reputation as major overachievers. From the mid-1940s on, Adams began getting more championship-caliber players, and the pieces of the most impressive teams in history began to fall into place.

In the fall of 1944, a 5'8" 150-pound teenager with a bum knee caught the coach's eye during a tryout. He was not the fastest or best player on the ice, but he was absolutely relentless. His name was Ted Lindsay, and he was the kind of player a team could build around. Lindsay had wanted to play for the Toronto Maple Leafs, but the team balked at his demand for a guarantee that he would never be sent to the minor leagues. The Red Wings believed the little guy had both the raw talent and mean-ness to become a valuable player, and they were correct. Indeed, some believe he was the best left wing ever to play the game. That same year Adams inked a hulking 16-year-old right wing to a contract and sent him to the minors for a couple of years of seasoning. His name was Gordie Howe. By the end of the decade, Lindsay and Howe would be playing on the same line with Abel and making hockey history. In the meantime, Detroit was signing and develop-ing other top youngsters, including centers Alex Delvecchio and Red Kelly, defense-man Marcel Pronovost, and goalie Terry Sawchuk. Much would be expected from this group during the 1950s.

The Early 1950s: Motor City Muscle

The concentration of talent in the NHL dur-ing the 1950s was unprecedented in the his-tory of professional sports. Never before or since had so many highly skilled athletes competed for so few spots in a pro league. Only six NHL teams existed between 1943 and 1966, and after Canada had fully recov-ered from World War II, there were hun-dreds of hockey players trying for the few spots that opened up on NHL rosters each year. The first half of the decade belonged to the Detroit Red Wings, while the second half belonged to the Montreal Canadiens. These clubs, which had tasted glory during the war years, had acquired a thirst for champagne, and each spring they waged an all-out battle for the right to sip it from the Stanley Cup.

Detroit first served notice that it meant to muscle its way to the top during the 1949 playoffs, when young Gordie Howe came of age. In the semifinals against the Cana-diens, he stole the spotlight from Rocket Richard with eight goals in seven games. The following season, Howe blossomed into a terrific scorer with 35 goals, which had quite an impact on his linemates. With Howe drawing so much attention, Sid Abel scored a career-high 34 goals, and Ted Lindsay was credited with a league-leading 55 assists—many of which came on shots that Howe tipped in. The two youngsters worked the corners like veterans; in the open ice they used the give-and-go with devastat-ing effectiveness. In 1949–50, Lindsay, Abel, and Howe finished 1-2-3 in the NHL in scoring, and by season's end everyone was calling them—in a nod both to Detroit's sta-tus as the capital of the automobile industry

As strong, skilled, and tough as any player in hockey history, Gordie Howe played NHL hockey in an incredible *five* decades. Over the course of his career he scored 1,850 points with 801 goals, put his name on three Stanley Cups, six Art Ross Trophies, and six Hart Trophies, and became known to all as Mr. Hockey.

and to the trio's prolific scoring—the Production Line.

No one could believe how good Howe had become. Great things had been predicted for him since the mid-1940s, but expectations had begun to drop a bit after he tallied only 103 points in three seasons. By the end of the 1949–50 season, however,

most players agreed that it would be only a matter of time before he supplanted Richard as the game's top right wing. Opponents already respected Howe for his strength and fighting ability, but he was now the kind of instinctive passer who could rip a defense apart, especially late in games when defensemen were a step slower and more apt to make mental mistakes. A dedicated player, Howe stayed after practice to work on his shooting skills, preferring to shoot when he was tired instead of when he was fresh. He also soaked up knowledge and strategy from Abel whenever he could. Soon Howe knew what to do—and how to do it—in almost every situation a player might encounter. He also knew how to get the room he needed to maneuver. Always on the move, he skated with his elbows out, daring opponents to shadow him. When they did, they paid dearly for it—over the years Howe probably caused more deep bruises and knocked out more teeth with "incidental" contact than any five ordinary players combined. Not surprisingly, by the third period of a game, no one wanted any part of Gordie Howe. And that, of course, was when he did a great deal of damage.

Behind the Production Line, Detroit finished first an astounding seven years in a row and won the Stanley Cup four times in six seasons beginning in 1949–50. For most of that period, the team's goaltending job was held down by Terry Sawchuk, who many still regard as the top man ever to put on the pads. His reflexes were otherworldly, enabling him to wait for the shooter to commit first—a luxury most angle-playing goalies do not have. At times, Sawchuk was impossible to beat. Indeed, he averaged a shutout every 10 games (103 in 971 contests),

Terry Sawchuk's intensity and lightning-quick reflexes were a major part of the Detroit Red Wings' dominance during the early 1950s.

Red Kelly used his brilliant play-making skills as a defenseman with Detroit and then as a center in his hometown of Toronto; over his 20-year career, he won four Cups apiece with the Red Wings and the Maple Leafs.

establishing a record that might never be broken.

Playing in front of Sawchuk were several top defensemen, including Leo Reise, Marcel Pronovost, shot-blocking specialist Bob Goldham, and the remarkable Red Kelly. Kelly was the man who made the Wings go. A former forward, he was an offensive defenseman who actually could play defense. That meant Kelly could break up a scoring threat, then turn the puck around and apply pressure on the opposite goal. He was also a gentleman, winning the Norris Trophy (as the league's best defender) and the Lady Byng Trophy (for sportsmanship) in the same season. One might think this unlikely combination would serve as an invitation for the NHL's top goons to pound on the gentlemanly Kelly, but Red was rarely picked on. He had been a light-heavyweight boxing champion while in college; no one wanted to find out if he still had his knockout punch. Another gentleman on the muscle-bound Red Wings was Alex Delvecchio. An excellent assist man, he centered for Detroit's second-tier scorers, including Metro

THE RICHARD RIOT

Aggression and physical intimidation are part of the landscape of hockey, but there have been many instances where the violent collisions and fisticuffs on the ice have gone way overboard or have sparked unruly behavior by fans. One of the ugliest incidents in hockey history occurred in the aftermath of a game in Boston during which Montreal's Maurice Richard lost his head, clobbering an unsuspecting Bruin with his stick and roughing up a linesman. NHL president Clarence Campbell immediately suspended Richard for the remainder of the season. Four days later, on March 17, 1955, Campbell was in attendance when the Canadiens hosted the hated Detroit Red Wings. The Montreal crowd was in a foul mood, with their top player banned and their team tied in the standing with the Wings.

Almost immediately, fans began throwing peanuts and rolled-up programs at Campbell, who was seated near the ice. After a while, this escalated into unruly behavior throughout the arena, and suddenly things got out of control. A smoke bomb was ignited behind one of the goals and thousands of people, thinking the building was on fire, stampeded for the exits. In the confusion, a group of fans barreled through the police line set up around Campbell, who held his ground. One individual stuck his hand out as if to shake the commissioner's hand, then pulled it back and sucker-punched him in the face. The game was forfeited—just the second time in league history that had happened.

Outside the Forum, a group of teenagers began whipping the crowd into a frenzy. Then someone shot out some of the windows in a nearby building. Minutes later a full-fledged mob began tearing up everything in sight. They moved through Montreal's downtown area breaking into department stores and destroying automobiles. It took a plea by Mayor Jean Drapeau to keep Campbell from attending Montreal's next home game and a radio address by Richard begging fans to "get behind the team" to avert further trouble.

Prystai, and was one of the most reliable and consistent all-around players in the league.

Detroit beat the Rangers in a wild seven-game final in 1950, with the Cup winner scored 28 minutes into overtime of the deciding game. After losing in the first round to Montreal in 1952, the Red Wings avenged this defeat the following spring by sweeping the Canadiens in the finals. Sawchuk was the big hero, limiting Richard and company to a measly two goals in four games. In 1953, Detroit lost a shocker to the Boston Bruins, who went on to get wiped out by the Canadiens. Finally, the Red Wings put it all together, winning consecutive Stanley Cups in 1954 and 1955. Both championships came in seven-game finals against the hated Canadiens, with the first settled in overtime and the second showcasing the talents of Howe, who by this time had emerged as the most valuable player in hockey.

The Late 1950s: Montreal's Historic Run

The Canadiens were far from finished, however. Although they had but one NHL title to show for their five consecutive trips to the Stanley Cup Finals, the team did not disintegrate following these disappointments. On the contrary, the Canadiens became even stronger. During the years of near misses, a new generation of players had

Montreal coach Toe Blake behind the bench. Blake spent the whole of his hockey life with the Canadiens: as a player he was a gifted left wing and member of the Punch Line with Rocket Richard and Elmer Lach; as coach he led the Habs to eight Cups in 13 years.

joined Montreal, and they had gained valuable postseason experience. The first big star to move up to the club was defenseman Doug Harvey; the second was Bernie Geoffrion. These two men set the stage for a transformation—both in the fortunes of the Canadiens and in the way hockey would be played.

Harvey was a brilliant defender who came into the league and simply decided the sport was being played incorrectly. An excellent stickhandler, he could pluck the puck off an opponent's stick, yet rarely lost it himself. This proficiency with the puck meant that when Harvey broke up a play, he was perfectly capable of moving up the ice and igniting the offense. This in turn meant the Montreal forwards did not have to skate back to take the puck, as was the custom of the day. After three periods, the Canadien wings usually had much fresher legs than their opponents. With the Montreal forwards free to do as they pleased, Harvey saw a whole new game unfold before him. Instead of a center bringing the puck over center ice with two forwards ahead of him, the Canadiens could send Harvey up as an attacker and have three scorers swooping in on goal. This may sound familiar to today's fans, but 50 years ago it was almost unheard of. Teams had to change the way they played Montreal, and at such a high level this was not an easy task.

In 1951, Bernie Geoffrion became a regular, and he added a new wrinkle to the Montreal offense: the slap shot. He was not the first to use it, but he was the first to control it, and the Canadiens were the first to run plays designed to kick the puck out to the blue line for a shot. Up until then, the idea was to work the puck in close for a wrist shot, a backhand, or a redirection.

Anything that skittered back toward the blue line gave goalies a chance to catch their breath. With Geoffrion blasting away from the point, opposing netminders were under constant assault and at constant risk of giving up long rebounds. Geoffrion scored about 30 goals a season from his post at right wing. He earned the nickname Boom-Boom for the noise he made while practicing in an empty rink.

The 1954–55 season saw the emergence of three more young Montreal superstars. Forwards Jean Beliveau and Dickie Moore worked their way into the regular rotation, and Jacques Plante replaced Gerry McNeil as Montreal's number-one goalie. Netminders have always been notoriously intense and eccentric, but the brainy, solitary Plante truly stood out as a breed apart. Plante's approach to hockey extended beyond his own net, and he broke what was then the cardinal rule of goaltending by regularly leaving his position. He was the first goalie to sprawl far out of the crease to cover loose pucks and the first to skate to the boards to control a dump-in. If Plante felt an opponent was going to beat his teammates to a loose puck, he would dart to the boards and either flick it out of the zone or set it up for his defensemen. Plante, whose nickname was Jake the Snake, won the Vezina Trophy five consecutive times beginning in 1955–56 and was also the man responsible for inventing the goalie's mask.

Dickie Moore was a left winger who could play right wing or center if a teammate was injured. He was the least glamorous member of hockey's marquee team, and he used this relative obscurity to his advantage. Moore worked the boards, forechecked, patrolled the slot, and never gave up on a play. While opponents were

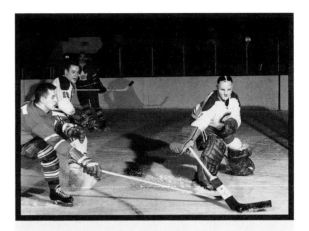

A Hall of Fame netminder, Jacques Plante was also the first goalie to wear a protective mask during an NHL game.

focused on one of his high-profile teammates, he often had room to score and set up goals. In 1958–59, he registered 96 points to set a record that held up until the league expanded. Fiercely proud, he played through excruciating knee, wrist, and shoulder injuries during his prime years and never complained.

Jean Beliveau was the most admired player of the postwar era. He was big, he was graceful, and he had a mind like a computer. Until Wayne Gretzky's arrival many years later, no one had the ability to size up a situation and think two passes ahead like Beliveau. Until Mario Lemieux came along, no one used his size and power as effectively as Beliveau. And no one has ever replaced him in the hearts of Montreal fans. The most sought-after junior player of his time, Beliveau came to the Canadiens just as injury and age were beginning to catch up to Maurice Richard. What the Rocket had lost in terms of scoring punch and physical intimidation Beliveau more than made

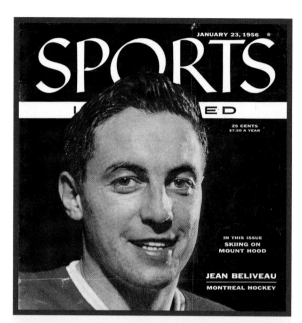

JANUARY 23, 1956

SPORTS
ED

25 CENTS
$7.50 A YEAR

IN THIS ISSUE
SKIING ON
MOUNT HOOD

JEAN BELIVEAU
MONTREAL HOCKEY

Big Jean Beliveau made many head-lines in the late 1950s, when he pushed the Canadiens to five straight Stanley Cups with smooth moves and intelligent play.

up for, leading the league in points and penalty minutes in 1955–56. He also provided the unwavering leadership the team had lacked for so long.

With this nucleus of Hall of Famers, the Montreal Canadiens put together hockey's first true dynasty. In the 1956 playoffs, under new coach Toe Blake, they blew past the Rangers 4–1 and ended Detroit's dominance with an easy five-game victory in the finals. Beliveau scored seven times against the Red Wings to cap off a spectacular year. Detroit was dumped in the first round of the 1957 playoffs, so the Canadiens faced the surprising Bruins in the finals. With Plante limiting Boston to a mere six goals, Montreal won the series 4–1 to take back-to-back Stanley Cups. As it turned out, they were just getting warmed up. In each of the

next three campaigns, the Canadiens finished first in the regular season and cruised through the playoffs to win the championship. During Montreal's amazing five straight Stanley Cups, the team stayed more or less intact, with the lone newcomer being Henri Richard, Maurice's little brother. He and Beliveau would form the nucleus of the franchise's next great team, as the stars of the 1950s were finally cut down by age, injuries, and trades during the early 1960s.

Toronto on Top Again

As the six-team era wound to a close—the NHL would undergo a radical expansion after the 1966–67 season—the dominant team in the NHL was still the Montreal Canadiens, who finished in first or second place every year. The Chicago Blackhawks also had an excellent team, winning the Stanley Cup in 1961 and developing marvelous players throughout the decade. The team that took four Stanley Cups in six years, however, was the Toronto Maple Leafs.

Just as they had in the 1940s, the Leafs found a way to turn it on come playoff time. Toronto had an excellent defensive corps led by Tim Horton, who was at the height of his powers in the early 1960s. He shared the ice with four other workhorse defenders, including veteran Red Kelly, Bob Baun, Allen Stanley, and Carl Brewer—each of whom played through injuries that would have put some players out for weeks. In goal was Johnny Bower, who had kicked around the minors since the end of World War II before landing a job with the Leafs in the late 1950s. He was the league's hardest-working goalie and a perfect complement to Horton and company.

HOCKEY'S COLOR LINE CRUMBLES

On January 18, 1958, the NHL became the last major-league sport to have its color line broken when Willie O'Ree skated onto the ice for the Boston Bruins. There had never been rules prohibiting people of color from playing in the NHL, but in the years following World War II, none of the dozen or so black stars in junior hockey had ever made the jump to the big time. O'Ree, a left wing, was a major talent—even after losing the sight in his right eye when he was hit by a puck as a teenager. His handicap kept him from being a star, and his initial stay in the NHL lasted only two games. However, O'Ree returned to the Bruins for the 1960–61 season and proved a valuable bit player.

O'Ree's significance was not lost on Bruin fans. When he scored his first goal on New Year's Day, 1961, he received a two-minute standing ovation from the crowd at Boston Garden. Though his NHL career was confined to his two seasons with Boston, O'Ree played pro hockey for 21 years, tallying 1,022 points for 11 different teams. He was the target of abuse both from fans and players—and had to fight more often than most hockey players—but unlike his fellow pioneers in football and basketball, O'Ree always had the support of his teammates. In 1998, he was hired by the NHL to run its new Hockey Diversity Task Force.

As minority involvement in hockey increases through special grassroots pro-

Willie O'Ree shoots past Montreal defenseman Tom Johnson in a 1961 game.

grams, the league has become very much aware that it is tapping into a potential gold mine of new talent and new fans. It is also sensitive to the fact that it has to clean up its act, as a couple of ugly, racially motivated on-ice incidents during the 1997–98 season clearly illustrated.

Toronto was not blessed with a lot of offensive talent, but the team had clutch players in center Dave Keon and left wing Frank Mahovlich. Keon was a master checker and a solid offensive player from whom the team could expect 50 to 60 points a season. Mahovlich was the most talented wing the Leafs had ever had, yet he never seemed to do enough to keep the fans and coach Punch Imlach happy. He could skate, pass,

MORE MIDCENTURY STARS

Though much of the Hall of Fame talent in the NHL of the 1950s belonged to the Red Wings and Canadiens, there were other noteworthy players around the league. Andy Bathgate was the best offensive forward who did not play for Detroit or Montreal, and Bill Gadsby and Tim Horton embraced Doug Harvey's philosophies and helped the role of the defenseman evolve. Bathgate, a right wing, made the Rangers a respectable team and a dangerous opponent after becoming a regular for the New Yorkers in 1954. He was good for 25 to 40 goals a season and was a superb playmaker. Gadsby, who became his teammate after a 1955 trade from the Blackhawks, was one of the league's few offensive-minded defenders. He was also as tough as they come, beating polio in 1952 and playing through 600 stitches to last in the NHL for 20 years.

Tim Horton was the most feared defender in the league. The Maple Leaf star played the body, not the puck—adventurous forwards who ventured into the Toronto zone tended to get squashed against the sideboards like bugs against a windshield. A good passer, skater, and shooter, he picked his spots when the Maple Leafs had the puck and was a major contributor to the team's offense right into the 1960s, when the Leafs experienced a big resurgence. Horton was not a large man, but he had the strength of a bear. When opponents tried to lure him into a fight, he would not exchange punches but instead employed the famous bone-crunching Horton Hug, which helped him lay down the law without having to take a seat in the penalty box.

stickhandle, and shoot with unusual grace for a big man, but on a defense-oriented team his skills sometimes went to waste. Even so, he was expected to score every night and at the very least hit 50 for the season. That never happened, and Toronto fans never forgave him for it. His teammates knew how good he was, as did the rest of the league, and that probably kept Mahovlich from going crazy. After leading the Leafs to four Stanley Cups, he was released from bondage and went on to have highly productive seasons for Detroit and Montreal in the 1970s.

The Maple Leafs beat the defending champion Blackhawks in 1962, then downed the Red Wings in five games to take the Cup in 1963. Toronto defeated Detroit again in the 1964 finals, an exciting seven-game affair. In 1967, Toronto returned to the finals to face the Montreal Canadiens, winners of the Stanley Cup in 1965 and 1966. Despite being old and outgunned, the Leafs stifled the Montreal attack and escaped with a marvelous six-game victory. The average age of the Maple Leafs was 31, and they needed old-timer Terry Sawchuk to spell Bowers in goal. Keon, the baby of the team at 28, was a defensive terror and won the Conn Smythe Trophy as playoff MVP despite scoring just two points in the series. The victory of the hockey graybeards over the souped-up Canadiens is still considered one of the grandest moments in Stanley Cup play. Unless, of course, you happen to live in Montreal. The Canadiens probably had their champagne on ice before the series started, and the Toronto victory is still hard to believe when the two teams are compared on paper.

Montreal: The Next Generation

Montreal had a monster team during the 1960s. Jean Beliveau was still one of the best players in the game, and Henri Richard had in many ways become more valuable than his brother had been. The Pocket Rocket made the players around him better by making sure they got the puck when they needed it and covering for them when they were out of position. He was a wonderful assist man, leading the NHL in that category twice, and a relentless worker at both ends. When Richard retired, he had 11 championships under his belt; among members of major North American sports teams, only he and Bill Russell of basketball's Boston Celtics won that many.

Montreal's supporting cast consisted of Yvan Cournoyer, John Ferguson, J. C. Tremblay, Jacques Laperriere, Bobby Rousseau, Ralph Backstrom, Dick Duff, and Gump Worsley. This team beat the Blackhawks in seven games to win the Stanley Cup in 1965 and took the Red Wings in six games to win again in 1966. After losing to Toronto in 1967, the Canadi-

ens added more talent—Serge Savard, Jacques Lemaire, and Rogie Vachon—and won two more Stanley Cups, in 1968 and 1969. The Canadiens were so deep by this time that they actually had future stars Danny Grant and Mickey Redmond wasting away on the bench.

Bobby Hull and the Blackhawks

In the early 1960s, the team that seemed destined to become the decade's best was the Chicago Blackhawks. The core of players developed by the team was simply remarkable, yet they managed to win just one Stanley Cup. The big star for the Hawks was left winger Bobby Hull, who established himself as the dominant player of the 1960s when he led the club to the 1961 Stanley Cup and tallied 50 goals during the 1961–62 season. Hull seemed too good to be true. He was handsome and charismatic, and he had outrageous talent. No one skated faster than Bobby Hull, and no one shot the puck harder. This lethal combination made for some of the most dramatic individual performances ever seen in hockey, drawing many new fans to the game. Until Hull's arrival most Americans had a hard time naming more than one or two hockey players. During the 1960s, a lot of Americans knew Bobby Hull, even if they did not know which team he played for. The Golden Jet was hockey's first marketable star, and although his teams often came up short, he seemed to shatter a new scoring record almost every year.

Hull's Chicago teammates included some of the finest players of the era. Stan Mikita, who began his NHL career as a thug, made one of the truly remarkable transformations

Two stalwarts of the early 1960s Chicago Blackhawks were goon-turned-model-citizen Stan Mikita and Glenn Hall, who pioneered the butterfly style of goal-tending and played in an eye-popping 502 straight games.

in the annals of sports. He returned from a game one night to find his two-year-old daughter still up watching television. She asked him why he spent so much of the game sitting (in the penalty box) when all the other daddies were playing. At that moment he decided to beat opponents with his skill instead of his fists. Almost immediately he became one of the best all-around players in the league. Mikita won the scoring title four times during a five-year span and was the first player to win the Art Ross, Hart, and Lady Byng Trophies in the same season. His linemates, Ken Wharram and Doug Mohns, ranked among the better players in the league, as did Dennis Hull, Bobby's brother.

The Chicago defense was also quite good, with Pierre Pilote leading a crew that featured fellow All-Stars Elmer Vasko and Pat Stapleton. In goal, Glenn Hall was as good a puck stopper as there was. He earned the nickname Mr. Goalie the hard way: by appearing in 502 straight games. Hall broke in with the Red Wings in the mid-1950s, then moved to Chicago, where he played for 10 years. He pioneered the butterfly style of goaltending, which gives a goalie maximum ice coverage with his pads. The technique works only if a player has quick hands because shooters invariably try to aim high. Hall's reflexes might have been the best ever, but his nerves were another matter. Hall got so nervous before games that he regularly threw up in the dressing room. As one teammate put it, his bucket should be in the Hall of Fame.

Despite all that talent, the Blackhawks of the 1960s managed only one Stanley Cup;

Bobby Hull, the Golden Jet. Hull's good looks, booming slap shot, and blazing speed helped make him the NHL's first marketable superstar.

as these players began scoring goals in bunches for the Bruins.

The League Expands

With every major sport in the throes of expansion during the 1960s, it seemed only logical for the National Hockey League to follow suit. Cities had been applying for new franchises since the end of World War II, but for one reason or another the league never acted upon the requests. In 1967, the decision was made to add six brand-new teams: the Los Angeles Kings, Minnesota North Stars, Oakland Seals, Philadelphia Flyers, Pittsburgh Penguins, and St. Louis Blues. The new teams were placed in their own division so that the best expansion club would be guaranteed a berth in the Stanley Cup Finals. This was a smart move, as it kept interest in the expansion clubs high all

their fans will forever debate the causes of their team's relative underachievement. Most people believe the missing link was right under the club's nose in the person of Phil Esposito, a big young center who could pass like a little man. The Blackhawks put him on Hull's line in the mid-1960s and told him to set up their superstar. Esposito did a decent job for three seasons, but after failing to score a point against the Maple Leafs in the 1967 playoffs, he was shipped to the Boston Bruins along with two underutilized forwards named Ken Hodge and Fred Stanfield. Chicago's blunder was soon evident

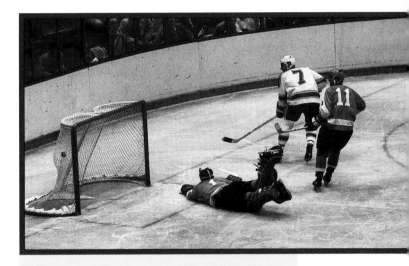

St. Louis Blues center Red Berenson pots the second of his six goals against the Flyers on November 7, 1968. His double hat trick still stands as a record for most goals scored in a road game.

year long. They got most of their players through a special draft and lured many retired stars back onto the ice with hefty contracts and a decent shot at playing for the Stanley Cup.

Among the future stars who got their first real shot with the expansion teams were forwards Bill Flett, Terry Crisp, Gary Dornhoefer, Danny Grant, Bill Goldsworthy, and Jean Pronovost; goalies Gerry Desjardins, Cesar Maniago, and Bernie Parent; and defensemen Carol Vadnais, Bill White, Joe Watson, and Bill, Bob, and Barclay Plager, who shared ice time for the St. Louis Blues. The best of the expansion clubs was St. Louis, which stocked its team with as many ex-Canadiens as they could find. Dickie Moore and Doug Harvey agreed to give it a go, as did former Montreal defensemen Jean-Guy Talbot and Jim Roberts. Collegiate legend Red Berenson, for whom

the Canadiens once had high hopes, was picked up by the Blues and became the star of the team. Behind the bench was Scotty Bowman, who had been coaching in the Montreal system since the 1950s. In goal was Glenn Hall, who had been acquired from Chicago. He was joined by former Canadien Jacques Plante in 1968–69.

More teams meant more games and more chances to shatter league scoring records. The schedule went from 70 to 74 games in 1967–68, then to 76 a year later. It reached 78 and then 80 during the first half of the 1970s. The first big record to be broken was the 100-point barrier. Bobby Hull and Stan Mikita had come close in the past, but the man who finally did it was their old teammate, Phil Esposito. Espo not only broke the record, he obliterated it, finishing the 1968–69 season with 126 points. Hull smashed the goal-scoring mark that season with 58, and Gordie

THE 1968 STANLEY CUP FINALS

As luck would have it, the Blues and Canadiens met for the 1968 Stanley Cup. St. Louis had barely edged the Flyers and North Stars in the first two rounds of the playoffs, so Montreal figured the finals were just a formality. What the Canadiens failed to realize, however, was that the Blues—whose coach and star players had come up in the Montreal system—knew everything there was to know about Canadien hockey. The first game went to the Canadiens in overtime, and the second game was a 1–0 win for Montreal. Game Three also went to Montreal, but they needed overtime again. Game Four was a 3–2 comeback win for the Canadiens, who completed the hardest sweep in hockey history. Hall was awarded the Conn Smythe Trophy for his heroic performance in goal. While his players were still celebrating their championship, Toe Blake announced his retirement, ending a remarkable era in NHL history.

Howe, at the age of 41, also broke the 100-point mark. Esposito's new record came on the strength of 77 assists, which established a single-season high.

This amazing performance heralded the arrival of a new and unusual superstar. Espo was like three great players stuffed into one body. He could control the tempo of a game with his stickhandling, much the way Doug Harvey had in his prime years with Montreal. Esposito liked things to move slowly. Although he had spent his formative years centering for speed demon Bobby Hull, it was his belief that if a game was played too quickly, a lot of easy opportunities would be missed. The second player in Esposito's body was the most obvious: He was a big, physical center who established position in

The Bruins' Phil Esposito shows off souvenirs from his record-setting fifth hat trick of the 1970–71 season. Espo piled up 76 goals that season, 18 more than the previous record.

front of the net and refused to relinquish it. A team could drag him down and take a penalty or try to keep him from scoring on tip-ins and rebounds. Neither strategy worked very well.

The third type of player taking up residence in Espo's #7 uniform was a cagey little playmaker—the kind who could skate in tight circles and then flick a no-look pass to a streaking teammate. This was the player that helped to beat teams time and again, for as soon as a defenseman came over to double up on Esposito, the puck was already on its way to the man he'd just left. He also had the stamina to take three- and four-minute shifts, which wore down defensemen and created all sorts of opportunities for Boston.

The Big Bad Bruins

Phil Esposito's arrival in Boston transformed a club that had already amassed some excellent talent under coach Harry Sinden, who was hired in 1966 after the Bruins failed to make the playoffs for the sixth straight season. Fred Stanfield gave the Bruins much-needed heft at center, while Ken Hodge turned his accurate shooting touch into one of the league's most feared weapons. Right wing Johnny Bucyk, Boston's all-time leading scorer up to that time, perked up with the arrival of Esposito and increased his output to better than a point a game. John McKenzie, a tough little right wing, was a rodeo star during the summers and a hatchet man for three other organizations before coming to Boston in 1966. With the Bruins he turned into an intelligent and combative goal scorer. Derek Sanderson, a hot-tempered star in junior hockey, was fast maturing into a solid offensive player. Ed

Westfall, an excellent defender, could play on the forward line and shadow an opponent's best player or drop back and function as a defenseman. Defenseman Ted Green, who skated on bad knees for most of his career, could hurt an opponent with his skill as a setup man or brawler. Don Awrey, who failed to make the NHL as a fast-skating, clean-checking defenseman, instead became an enforcer and fit right into the Boston style. Dallas Smith, a conservative stay-at-home defender, was also a veteran of the minor-league wars. In goal was Gerry Cheevers, a legendary lacrosse player who had spent almost 10 years in the minors before proving he was ready to handle NHL goaltending responsibilities.

The man who benefited most from the arrival of Esposito was Bobby Orr, who was on the verge of becoming the best player in the NHL. Orr was unlike anything anyone had ever seen on skates. He was the fastest, strongest, and most aggressive skater of his time. He was also a tremendous passer and great shooter. What made Orr so special, however, was the position to which he brought his immense talent: defenseman. For nearly a century, hockey teams moved players who were too old, were too slow, or had below-average shooting skills to the defensive end, where their deficiencies would be masked and they would not get in the way of the offensive players. Orr shattered this mold. He became a fourth forward, collecting the puck behind his own net and then steaming toward the enemy goal. Orr regularly beat opposing forwards down the ice, creating advantages for the Bruins and throwing a befuddling change of pace at opponents, who were struggling to adjust to Esposito's slowdown style. Orr further confused defenses because they never knew

whether he would pull up and pass or keep on going right to the net. No one in history handled the puck more during a game than Orr, and no one ever figured out a way to properly defend him.

The Bruins became an offensive juggernaut as Esposito and Orr matured and the veterans around them perfected their complementary roles. In 1969–70, Orr scored 33 goals and dished out an eye-popping 87 assists to lead the league in points. Right behind him was Esposito, with 43 goals and 56 assists. The Bruins beat the Rangers in

Boston's Gerry Cheevers, wearing his famous Stitch mask—he drew the stitches on to indicate what he'd look like he if were not wearing the mask—drops down to corral a shot.

THE FASTEST MAN ON SKATES: BOBBY ORR

The key to Bobby Orr's offensive ability was his skating. He could accelerate so quickly and maintain his balance so well that he sometimes seemed to defy the laws of physics. Just when an opponent thought he was going at full speed, he would crank it up a couple of notches. This made him almost impossible to check and gave him a huge advantage as a penalty killer. When the Bruins were defending against an enemy power play, Orr would collect the puck and simply skate circles around opponents until two or three converged on him and forced him to give it up. Sometimes he would fool them and suddenly wheel around, exploding away from his startled attackers to create a shorthanded breakaway.

Orr played defense because he was a tremendous checker and shot blocker and an excellent position player. He could see plays developing as a defender just as well as he could as an attacker. Orr also gave the Bruins another important defensive advantage: Teams were reluctant to send their forwards in deep against Boston because if Orr scooped up a loose puck, they would be completely outmanned at the other end. On a mediocre team, Orr's talents might have been wasted. But the Boston Bruins were an excellent club that always had at least one other offensive weapon on the ice.

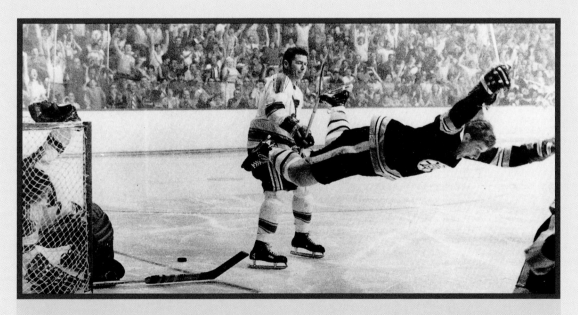

Boston's Bobby Orr levitates after scoring the goal that finished the St. Louis Blues in the 1971 Stanley Cup Finals.

the first round of the playoffs, swept the Blackhawks in the semifinals, and then destroyed the St. Louis Blues in four games to win the Stanley Cup. Orr scored the clincher 40 seconds into overtime, swooping in on goal and blasting the puck past Glenn Hall. It was Boston's first Cup in 29 years.

The following season saw the Bruins dominate the NHL. The team won 57 games and scored 108 more goals than the league's second-best offense. Orr had a season for the ages, with 37 goals and an unprecedented 102 assists. Many of those assists set up Esposito goals; in all, the burly center netted 76 to establish a new record. He also doled out 76 assists to set a new record for points in a season with 152. Finishing third and fourth in the NHL scoring race were fellow Bruins Bucyk and Hodge, with 116 and 105 points, respectively. Also in the top 10 were McKenzie, Stanfield, and left winger Wayne Cashman.

Not surprisingly, everyone in hockey was handing the 1971 Stanley Cup to the Bruins. But in the first round of the playoffs, Boston ran into a young goaltender who redefined the meaning of "hot." With a couple of weeks to go in the season, the Montreal Canadiens decided to give their regular netminder, Rogie Vachon, a breather. The team called up Ken Dryden from the minors. He played six games and demonstrated he could handle the pressure; the decision was made to start him against the Bruins in the playoffs. Seven games later, the Canadiens had disposed of the big bad Bostonians and Dryden was on his way to becoming a hockey legend. Montreal was in a period of transition, with Jean Beliveau in his last season and a lot of young players still a couple of years away.

But with Dryden keeping them in games they should have lost, the Canadiens marched all the way to the Stanley Cup, downing the Blackhawks in a dramatic seven-game final. He was awarded the Conn Smythe Trophy as postseason MVP, then won the Calder Trophy as the NHL's top rookie the following year—the only time that has ever happened.

The Broad Street Bullies

The Bruins won the 1972 Stanley Cup, defeating the up-and-coming Rangers in six games, and the Canadiens won it all in 1973, again beating Chicago. But the team that dominated play in the mid-1970s turned out to be the Philadelphia Flyers, an ugly, brawling bunch who took the NHL title in 1974 and 1975 with a little bit of skill and a lot of intimidation. The star of this team—the first of the expansion franchises to mature into a legitimate first-rate club—was center Bobby Clarke.

Clarke, who would win the Hart Trophy three times, was the finest on-ice leader of his era. He was a scrappy, hard-nosed player who outhustled and outmuscled opponents for loose pucks, getting amazing results from hockey skills that were barely above average. If a fellow player was in a slump, Clarke would get coach Fred Shero to put that man on his line until he had rebuilt his confidence. If the Flyers needed to take an opposing player out, it was Clarke who usually did the dirty deed. Because the team was stocked with brawlers, Clarke could get away with these actions; anyone who messed with the Philadelphia captain could expect immediate retribution. Clarke did excel in a couple of traditional roles—

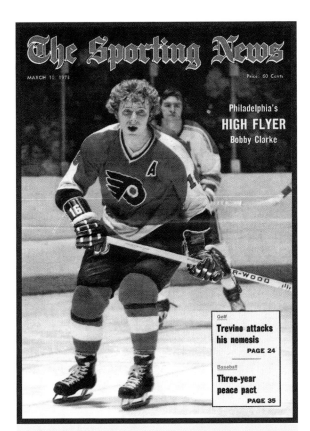

Bobby Clarke, the fiery, hard-nosed leader of the Broad Street Bullies of the mid-1970s, had his Flyers on the rise at the time of this 1973 issue of *The Sporting News.*

Dave Schultz, at home in the center of this fracas, embodied the ends-justify-the-means tactics of Philadelphia's evil-tempered championship teams. The Hammer was the Flyers' chief instrument of intimidation—he spent a record 472 minutes in the penalty box in 1974–75.

he was a superb face-off man and an excellent penalty killer—but it was as the toothless, stick-wielding leader of the Broad Street Bullies that he piled up his Hall of Fame credentials.

The Flyers did also boast some more mainstream talent. Goalie Bernie Parent had terrific reflexes and one of the fastest glove hands in history. He was spectacular during Philadelphia's two Stanley Cup drives, winning the Conn Smythe Trophy each time. Left wing Bill Barber burst onto the scene as a solid 30-goal scorer in the early 1970s, while Reggie Leach provided

scoring punch from the opposite side. Centering the team's second line was Rick MacLeish, who was good for 30 to 50 goals a season. When the Flyers needed to stir up trouble, they invariably turned to Dave Schultz and Bob Kelly, nicknamed the Hammer and the Hound, respectively.

Lafleur and the New Canadiens

The Flyers seemed destined to win a third straight championship in 1976, after leading the league in goals and surviving a season without Bernie Parent, who played in just 11 games. But Philadelphia ultimately ran into the Montreal Canadiens, who had been amassing a staggering collection of talent during the 1970s following the retirement of its Cup-winning stars of the 1960s. This outfit might well have been the best in NHL history. They humiliated the Flyers in four straight to win the 1976 Stanley Cup, then proceeded to fashion the league's best record each season from 1976–77 to 1978–79, winning 60, 59, and 52 games, respectively.

The defensive stars of this team were Ken Dryden and Larry Robinson. Dryden proved that his playoff performance in 1971 was not a fluke as he emerged as the game's most important goaltender during the mid-1970s. He studied and analyzed the game, preparing himself differently for each opponent. A large man for his position, he was unusually quick on his feet and used his

Ken Dryden, the Montreal Canadiens' superlative goalie of the 1970s, at eye level with a loose puck.

pads to make saves that other goalies could not. Dryden covered so much of the goal that he actually intimidated shooters. Of course, to get a decent shot on Dryden you had to get past Robinson, who was also an exceptionally large player at 6′4″. Using his long reach to poke check and contain enemy skaters, Big Bird could also lay a body on an opponent and put him right out of the game. This imposing physical presence was enough for Robinson to maintain order without resorting to fisticuffs. Working either with Guy Lapointe or Serge Savard, Robinson created a nearly impenetrable last line of defense, allowing the Montreal sharpshooters to swarm around the other team's goalmouth without fear of letting a break go the other way. Those sharpshooters included Steve Shutt, Pete Mahovlich, Jacques Lemaire, and Yvan Cournoyer—each of whom could put the puck in the net or set up a scoring opportunity with a nice move or a perfectly placed pass.

The most magnificent star on this magnificent team was Guy Lafleur, an offensive player held in such high regard by his peers that many called him the greatest ever to lace up a pair of skates. He played the game at two speeds—fast and faster—and rarely had more than just a general idea of what he would do next. This made him impossible to contain, for he might try anything at any time, and he rarely did the same thing twice. It was Lafleur's love of hockey, however, that set him apart from other high-scoring forwards. As a child he would sleep in his equipment, and as a pro he would suit up for games three to four hours before it was time to hit the ice. To Lafleur the rink was a canvas waiting for his master strokes; he felt it was both his right and responsibility to make each game a unique work of art.

After three so-so seasons with the Canadiens, Lafleur came into his own in 1974–75 with 53 goals and 119 points. Incredibly, that was the worst season he would have until a strained knee ligament slowed him down in 1980. Over a six-year span, Lafleur averaged 54 goals and 128 points. He won the Hart Trophy twice, led the league in scoring three times, and was honored as a first-team All-Star on six occasions.

The Canadiens rarely played a bad game in the late 1970s, and this included the postseason, where the team was almost unbeatable. Under coach Scotty Bowman—who had returned to Montreal after guiding the Blues to three Stanley Cup Finals—the

The Stanley Cup is paraded through Montreal's streets in celebration of the Canadiens' 1978 championship season. In all of team sports only baseball's New York Yankees rival the Canadiens' winning tradition; both teams have reached the pinnacle more than 20 times.

Guy Lafleur electrified Montreal fans time and again with his speed, twisty moves, and nose for the goal.

Canadiens followed their 1976 sweep of the Flyers with a sweep of the Bruins in the 1977 finals, a 4–2 win over Boston in 1978, and a 4–1 thrashing of the Rangers in 1979 to win a fourth consecutive Stanley Cup.

Stars of the 1970s

The 1970s might have been an era dominated by the Bruins, Flyers, and Canadiens, but thanks to expansion it also produced an unprecedented number of high-scoring stars. The New York Rangers boasted one of the most productive threesomes of all time in Jean Ratelle, Rod Gilbert, and Vic Hadfield. Nicknamed the GAG line (Goal-a-Game), it was a classic meshing of talents. Ratelle, the center, was a wonderful stickhandler and passer who also possessed a wicked wrist shot. Gilbert, at right wing, was a fast-skating slap-shot artist who averaged 30 goals a season during the 1970s. Hadfield was the hard-nosed garbage man who dug the puck out of the corners and hung around the crease waiting to bang in loose pucks. This trio accounted for 139 goals in 1971–72, catapulting the Rangers to their first Stanley Cup Finals in more than two decades.

In Buffalo, the expansion Sabres put together a talented trio in Gilbert Perrault, Rick Martin, and Rene Robert. Nicknamed the French Connection, this line brought the Sabres to the Cup Final in 1975, where they were edged by the Flyers in six games.

Perrault was the finest stickhandler of the decade, weaving his way past the slow-footed brutes who populated the NHL and creating scoring chances for his two wings, who topped the 40-goal mark a combined seven times.

Another player who became a superstar for an expansion club was Marcel Dionne, who began his career with the Red Wings in the early 1970s. Mismanagement and foolish trades gutted that club, so when Dionne's contract expired in 1975 he signed with the Los Angeles Kings. L.A. looked to be a team on the rise. Unfortunately, the Kings proceeded to trade away their high draft choices, and for the remainder of the decade they struggled to win. What success they did enjoy they owed to their diminutive center, who made up for ordinary skating skills with near-flawless stickwork. Despite being targeted by the league's goons,

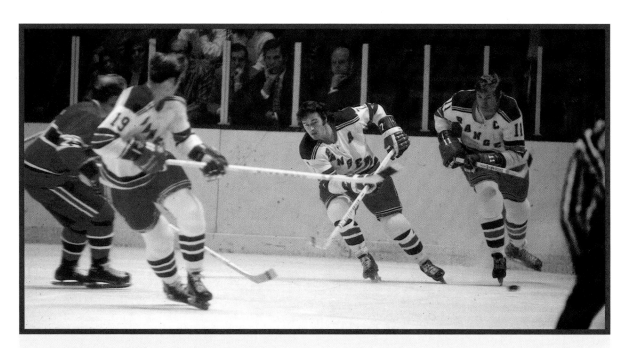

The New York Rangers' Goal-a-Game line starts a fast break. From left, Jean Ratelle, Rod Gilbert, and Vic Hadfield.

Dionne managed to net 50 or more goals an amazing six times.

The Toronto Maple Leafs fared a bit better than the Kings during the 1970s but never had enough offense to survive for more than a round or two in the playoffs. They did, however, possess Darryl Sittler, one of hockey's preeminent players from the mid-1970s on. A strong, aggressive player with tremendous leadership qualities, he ranked just behind Esposito and Clarke among the league's centers. He signed a huge deal and was named captain after Dave Keon went to the WHA, but the young Leafs never matured into the kind of team Keon led in the 1960s. Still, Sittler had some of the most remarkable games of the 1970s, including a 10-point performance against the Bruins in 1976 and a 5-goal

game in the playoffs. Later that year he starred for Team Canada in the first Canada Cup, scoring the tournament winner against Czechoslovakia in overtime.

The 1970s also saw the emergence of a new breed of defenseman. Bobby Orr did not have an equal, but he had several talented imitators. The two best were Brad Park and Denis Potvin. Park had the acceleration and shooting touch of a high-scoring forward and the toughness of a street brawler. He was a reckless and daring defender during his years with the Rangers and a solid, smart performer after a 1976 trade to the Bruins, where he replaced an injured Orr. Potvin came into the league with the New York Islanders in 1973 after shattering Orr's scoring record in junior hockey. Like Orr, he preferred to lead the charge, with the

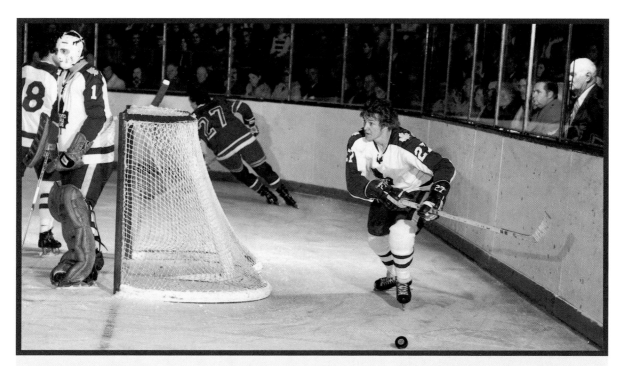

One of the NHL's top centers of the 1970s, Toronto's Darryl Sittler scored an amazing 10 points in a 1976 game against Boston, a feat unlikely to be duplicated.

SHOWDOWN AT THE SUMMIT

In the early 1970s, a great debate raged among international hockey fans. Were Canadian players the best in the world, or had the Soviet Union caught up? The thought that the Russians had somehow eclipsed NHL players seemed absurd to fans in North America, but for more than a decade the USSR had dominated Canadian amateurs in international play. Of course, the Soviet amateurs were not amateurs at all—they were paid professionals who spent little or no time working at regular jobs.

In September 1972, a special series was held between Team Canada and the Soviet National Team. The first four games were held in Canada, and the results shocked the hockey world.

The Soviets, behind the stellar goaltending of Vladislav Tretiak and the brilliant play of Valeri Kharlamov, Alexander Yakushev, and Boris Mikhailov, held a 2–1–1 lead. The series moved to Moscow, where Team Canada lost again to find itself on the brink of elimination. Here was a team featuring future Hall of Famers Phil Esposito, Frank Mahovlich, Rod Gilbert, and Brad Park, and they were getting creamed by a bunch of guys named Boris!

In one of hockey's great turnarounds, it was Paul Henderson—perhaps the least-known member of Team Canada—who bedeviled the Russians in the last three games to salvage the honor of the NHL. The veteran Maple Leaf left wing scored the tiebreaking goal in each of the final three contests, including knocking in his own rebound with 34 seconds left in Game Eight.

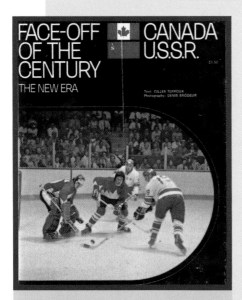

FACE-OFF OF THE CENTURY
THE NEW ERA
Text: GILLES TERROUX
Photography: DENIS BRODEUR

CANADA U.S.S.R.
$1.50

The 1972 Summit Series between the Soviet National Team and Team Canada marked the true beginning of hockey's international era—although Canada eked out a narrow come-from-behind victory, the Russians were clearly on a par with the cream of the Canadian-dominated NHL.

forward line flanking him as he streaked into the offensive zone. Islander coach Al Arbour spent years trying to convince Potvin that he would be more effective trailing plays, and when he finally caught on to this tactic the team was transformed into a powerhouse. Potvin was a legitimate 30-goal scorer, an excellent passer, and a devastating body checker. Of all the offensive defensemen who have come along since Orr hit the scene, Potvin has come the closest to matching his all-around talent.

THE WORLD HOCKEY ASSOCIATION

For seven years during the 1970s, there was a second major hockey league in operation. Its name was the World Hockey Association, and it was the brainchild of the two men who launched the American Basketball Association—Dennis Murphy and Gary Davidson. The WHA started in 1972, with clubs in 12 cities. The new league went head-to-head with NHL franchises in Philadelphia, New York, Los Angeles, Minnesota, and Chicago and split its remaining six franchises between U.S. and Canadian cities. It got off with a bang, signing the NHL's most popular player, 33-year-old Bobby Hull, and its most famous player, Gordie Howe, who came out of retirement at the age of 46 to play with his two teenage sons, Mark and Marty. Following these Hall of Famers were other NHL stars, including Derek Sanderson, Ted Green, Dave Keon, Gerry Cheevers, and Frank Mahovlich.

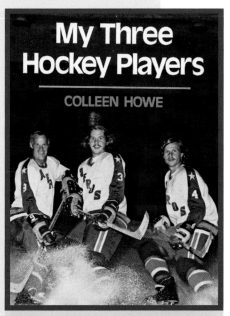

Gordie Howe came out of retirement to join his sons Marty (left) and Mark on the Houston Aeros, giving the World Hockey Association an instant star attraction.

For many years, NHL owners had managed to convince their players that they were not making any money. But with expansion it became clear that there was a tremendous amount of money to be made in pro hockey. This fact was driven home by the contract signed by Bobby Orr in 1966, which was triple the amount of the next highest salary. During the next few years, players began earning more, but they harbored a lot of resentment for the injustices of the 1960s. When the chance came to play the NHL millionaires against the WHA millionaires, many players did so—to both their enrichment and delight.

The early stars of the WHA were scoring sensation Andre Lacroix and Howe. Hull, who played for the Winnipeg Jets, scored 77 goals in 1974–75. Nilsson and Hedberg went on to be stars for the New York Rangers in the early 1980s. In the mid-1970s, Marc Tardif, Real Cloutier, and Robbie Ftorek emerged as stars.

The 1978–79 season would be the WHA's last. More than two dozen franchise shifts in seven years had exhausted fans trying to follow the league, and emptied the pockets of the once-enthusiastic owners. Interest in hockey had grown during the 1970s, but hockey itself had grown too big. The NHL had moved into five new cities since the original expansion in 1967, while the WHA had 32 teams in 24 different towns at various times. The NHL had been extending an olive branch to the WHA since the mid-1970s, holding discussions about a potential merger. When the WHA went out of business, the NHL brought in 4 of the remaining 6 franchises— bringing the league to 21 teams for the 1979–80 season.

The Early 1980s: Reign of the Islanders

As the 1980s began, several forces were at work in hockey. When the World Hockey Association folded, the National Hockey League gained dozens of young players who had honed their skills on the major-league level. This sudden infusion of talent raised the level of play in the NHL almost immediately. So, too, did the growing presence of European stars, who had been lured to North America during the salary wars between the NHL and WHA. Their wide-open style was perfect for the WHA and also won converts in the NHL, where the Montreal Canadiens had proved that you could win Stanley Cups without resorting to grind-it-out hockey. Tough, rugged defense and clutch goaltending still decided games, but a swarming quick-strike offense was clearly the way hockey was headed.

This played right into the hands of Al Arbour and the New York Islanders, who had assembled an excellent team by the end of the 1970s. Denis Potvin led a solid defensive corps while Billy Smith established himself as the most competitive and combative goalie in the game. The offense was led by one of the best lines in history, consisting of center Bryan Trottier, left wing Clark Gillies, and right wing Mike Bossy. Trottier was the kind of player coaches dreamed of. He was strong enough to lay out an opponent yet had a soft touch when delivering the puck to a teammate. When players began crunching into each other, Trottier seemed always to know where the puck would squirt out; he initiated countless scoring plays this way. Gillies was the digger, using his huge body to outmuscle opponents for loose pucks along the boards

Denis Potvin, a defenseman who added bone-crunching checking to Bobby Orr–like offensive skills, captained the New York Islanders throughout their reign in the early 1980s.

and establishing position around the net while Trottier and Potvin swirled around the rink. A remarkable big-game performer and a strong and accurate shooter, he was regarded by many as the most valuable all-around left wing to come into the game since Bobby Hull.

Mike Bossy was more one-dimensional than his linemates, but that one dimension accounted for a goal-scoring spree that might never again be matched. The right winger was hockey's all-time opportunist, waiting for that one moment when a defenseman let up or turned away for just an instant. When this happened, Bossy would sprint for an open spot, take a pass from a teammate, and in one flawless motion send the puck humming toward the net. He was fast and he was accurate, but what enabled him to score 50 or more goals in each of his first nine NHL seasons was a deceptiveness that drove goalies insane. Bossy was the only player, they insisted, whose shot could not be read. Until the puck was on its way, you did not know if Bossy was going high, low, left, or right . . . until it was too late.

Behind this marvelous threesome was a group of heady, opportunistic offensive players, including speedy Bob Bourne, tough John Tonelli, and veteran center Butch Goring. The Isles even had a talented group of European players, led by Stefan Persson, Bob Nystrom, and Anders Kallur. And whatever spare part the team needed general manager Bill Torrey secured before playoff time rolled around.

The Islanders reached the Stanley Cup Finals for the first time in 1980. They defeated the Philadelphia Flyers, who had reassembled themselves into a more balanced club with the development of forwards Brian Propp, Mel Bridgman, Ken Linseman, and Paul Holmgren. Bobby Nystrom scored the Cup winner in overtime of Game Six, while Trottier took home the Conn Smythe Trophy. In 1981, the Isles dominated in the regular season and swept through the playoffs without a scare. Goring starred in the five-game victory over the Minnesota North Stars in the finals while Bossy set postseason records with 35 points and nine power-play goals.

No U.S.-based team had ever won three straight Stanley Cups, but in 1981–82 the smart money was on the Islanders to repeat as NHL champions. As the season progressed, however, the Edmonton Oilers loomed as a major threat to this quest. Wayne Gretzky, already recognized as the league's best player, was rewriting the record books, averaging better than a goal a game. But to the shock of Oilers fans, Edmonton was dumped in the first round by the Kings. This all but guaranteed the Islanders another Cup, for there was not a single team on the other side of the draw with a winning record. After disposing of the Rangers and Quebec Nordiques, the Islanders faced the Vancouver Canucks, whom they swept with relative ease to win a third consecutive NHL championship. The Oilers did reach the finals in 1983, but again their fans were stunned when they lost four straight to the Islanders, who became only the second franchise in history to win four consecutive Cups. Billy Smith was spectacular in limiting the high-scoring Oilers—who had averaged more

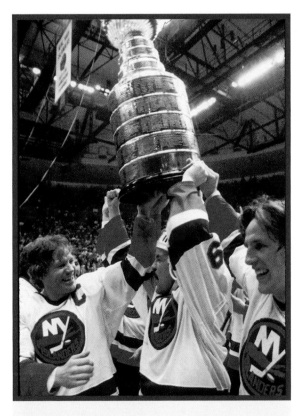

Brian Trottier holds the Stanley Cup aloft after the Islanders clinched their second of four straight championships.

THE GREAT GRETZKY

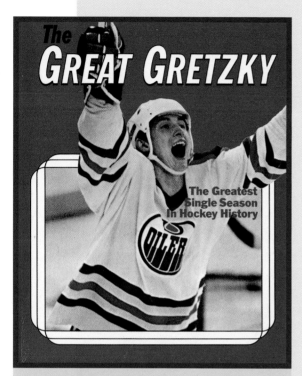

Slightly built but possessed of other-worldly playmaking instincts, Wayne Gretzky has rewritten nearly all of hockey's single-season and career scoring records. This book commemorated his astounding 1981–82 season: He scored 50 goals in his first 39 games, then finished the year with 92 goals and 212 points.

In the final days of the World Hockey Association, the wheeler-dealers were moving quickly to cash in on what few opportunities remained. The smartest of the bunch was Nelson Skalbania, who owned the Indianapolis Racers. Hoping to turn his team's fortunes around, Skalbania signed Canada's hottest product, 17-year-old Wayne Gretzky, to a personal services contract.

Every team in hockey knew about Gretzky, but the rules of the WHA and NHL forbade the drafting of a player prior to his 18th birthday. Skalbania's shrewd move beat everyone to the punch, but to his dismay it did not save his WHA franchise. When he went to local businesses to sell season tickets to watch the greatest young player in the game, he discovered that no one in Indianapolis had ever heard of Gretzky. Skalbania realized that he would have to sell Gretzky to a team in a city that understood the teenager's value. The two healthiest franchises in the WHA were the Edmonton Oilers and the Winnipeg Jets, and he held an auction between the two for Gretzky's services. Oiler owner Peter Pocklington made the winning bid. Skalbania pocketed a large sum of cash, folded his team, and walked away a winner.

Meanwhile, the Gretzky Era had begun. He led Edmonton to a first-place finish with 46 goals and

than five goals per game during the regular season—to six goals in four games.

The Oilers Rise to the Top

After two shocking disappointments, the Edmonton Oilers were either going to dominate the NHL or self-destruct. They wanted a Stanley Cup in the worst way, and they prayed that they would get another crack at the Islanders. The Isles obliged, winning three tough series to reach the finals in 1984. The Oilers survived a second-round scare against Calgary to fulfill their end of the bargain. After the teams split the

64 assists in 1978–79 and continued his brilliant play when the Oilers moved to the NHL the following season. A skinny six-footer with wavy blond hair and a baby face, Gretzky caught the league by surprise when he tallied a league-high 86 assists and won the Art Ross Trophy with 137 points.

There was something very different about the way he played hockey; no one had ever seen anything like him before. Gretzky was not the fastest skater or the fanciest stickhandler, yet somehow he managed to weave into the open just as the puck arrived or put a perfect pass on a teammate's stick without making him break stride. He was not the hardest shooter, yet when given just an inch or two of open goal, he managed to put the puck in the net. Gretzky was proving that hockey was a mental game. He seemed to be thinking two or three passes ahead of everyone else and processing extraordinary amounts of visual information in fractions of a second. Gretzky was sometimes compared to a sparrow who could swoop at 30 miles an hour toward a hurricane fence, pull its wings in just in time to shoot through the links, and then continue flying on the other side. Indeed, he often claimed the game around him seemed to go into slow motion at times, giving him a good long look at things that other players never noticed.

In his second NHL season, Gretzky dished out 109 assists and set a new record with 164 points. In 1981–82, he scored an all-time record 92 goals, reaching the 50-goal plateau before even half the season had passed. He also won his third of eight consecutive Hart Trophies as NHL MVP. In 1983–84, he got a goal or assist in 51 straight games, and in 1985–86 he registered 163 assists and 215 points. By the end of the 1980s, Gretzky was being hailed as the greatest team-sport athlete in history—above Babe Ruth, Jim Brown, and Wilt Chamberlain—and had changed forever the way hockey teams played offense and defense, and how much hockey players were paid.

first two games, Edmonton took over, easily winning the final three to become the first ex-WHA franchise to win the Stanley Cup.

What enabled the Oilers to succeed where they had so often failed? It was a combination of three things. First, Mark Messier matured into a tough and charismatic team leader. Second, Edmonton's goalie, Grant Fuhr, was the kind of player who rose to meet the pressure of big games. And third, Gretzky's talented teammates, who had had a tendency to stand around admiring him along with the rest of the hockey world, began to fulfill their own immense potential.

Mark Messier, a gritty, gifted center, was a major part of the Edmonton Oilers' success during the 1980s.

The 1983–84 Edmonton Oilers were a special team. They not only had six of the most talented players in NHL history, but each was in his prime. Messier joined the Oilers as a teenager and quickly learned how to put his size, finesse, and intelligence into action, becoming one of the most feared players in the league. On offense, he was an above-average puckhandler and passer, but he could also muscle his way to the net. His wrist shot, delivered perfectly in stride, enabled him to become a big scorer. Messier made All-NHL at left wing, although he excelled at center and even on right wing. His brute strength made him a formidable defender, especially when it came to clearing opponents out of the slot. What coach Glenn Sather loved most about Messier, however, was the fire in his eyes. In big games, he got the Look—the same expression Rocket Richard wore when Stanley Cup time rolled around.

By 1983–84, Messier had assumed leadership of the Oilers, relieving Gretzky of this burden and making teammates think twice about not giving 100 percent. Not that this was a problem. Certainly not with Jari Kurri and Glenn Anderson. Kurri, who hailed from Finland, joined the Oilers in 1980 and soon became the right wing on Gretzky's line. A smooth skater with excellent timing on his shot, Kurri worked beautifully with the Great One. Each knew where the other would be, and at times they seemed to be playing a game within a game to see who could make the best cut, the nicest pass, or the quickest shot.

Anderson combined great feet, great hands, and great balance with tremendous speed to become one of the game's most unique left wingers. Rather than shying away from contact—as most quick players do—Anderson actually looked to initiate it. He knew that if he plowed into an opponent, he would recover more quickly, thus giving the Oilers the advantage. Not surprisingly, he gained a reputation as a kamikaze, but his Oiler teammates knew better: Anderson sometimes looked as if he were out of control, but he almost always had a plan. He was good for 35 to 55 goals a season, and although his assist totals were somewhat low, he contributed mightily to Edmonton goals in ways that never made it into the box scores.

Defenseman Paul Coffey and goalie Grant Fuhr represented Edmonton's defense, although Coffey was more renowned as an offensive player. In an end-to-end race, he might have been the team's fastest skater, and he used this speed to join the Oiler attack whenever an opportunity presented itself. Often compared to Bobby Orr, Coffey might have been a stride slower and a little less agile, but he was just as good at putting the puck in the net and even better at the long outlet pass. With Gretzky, Kurri, and Anderson breaking out in front of him, these deliveries often turned into goals; in his seven seasons with the Oilers, Coffey topped 120 points an amazing three times. Fuhr, a stand-up goalie with terrific reflexes, replaced Andy Moog as the team's number-one netminder in 1983–84 and just got better and better. Fuhr was a master at cutting down shooting angles, which was important because the offensive-minded Oilers did give their opponents good scoring opportunities. Fuhr was also an excellent skater, which meant he could leave the net and chase down loose pucks and still get back to the crease quickly. Fuhr also took advantage of Edmonton's scoring prowess by whipping pucks up ice to his forwards. When opponents swarmed around his net, he could go down butterfly style without worrying about high shots, for he had the quickest glove hand in the NHL.

Wayne Gretzky goes to work behind the net. So coolly does Gretzky pick apart defenses from this part of the ice with deft stickhandling and perfect passes that it has become known as his office.

With this core of players, Edmonton management needed only to keep the team supplied with smart, tough role players. They did this by adding Mike Krushelnyski, Esa Tikkanen, Craig MacTavish, Marty McSorley, Craig Simpson, and Reijo Ruotsalainen over the next few years to a supporting cast that already included Kevin Lowe, Charlie Huddy, and Dave Semenko. The Oilers repeated as Stanley Cup champions in 1985 with a five-game victory over the Philadelphia Flyers and won it all again in 1987 and 1988.

Prior to the 1988–89 season, Edmonton owner Peter Pocklington, strapped for cash, sent Gretzky to the Los Angeles Kings in a deal that brought back draft choices and more than $15 million. This seemingly signaled the end of the Edmonton dynasty. With Gretzky traded and Coffey lost to free agency, there seemed little hope of another championship. As if to confirm this suspicion, the Oilers were defeated in the playoffs by Gretzky's Kings in the spring of 1989. But in 1989–90, Messier pushed his game up another notch, and the Oilers won their fifth Stanley Cup in seven years. Not only did Mess win the Hart Trophy as league MVP, he put to rest any doubt about who the heart of the Oilers was during their glory years.

Stars of the Wide-Open 1980s

Although the 1980s were dominated by the Islanders and Oilers, several other franchises put excellent teams on the ice. The Philadelphia Flyers reached the Stanley Cup Finals three times and developed several top players, including Tim Kerr, Rick Tocchet, WHA refugee Mark Howe, and goalie Ron

GOING FOR THE GOLD

Ice hockey has a long history at the Winter Olympics, debuting during the 1920 games in Antwerp, Belgium. As one might expect, the Canadian national squad dominated the competition at first, taking the gold medal in 1920, 1924, 1928, and 1932.

Instead of collecting its best amateurs and training them as a group, Canada took the whole of its best amateur team to the Olympics. Regardless of who suited up, though, Canada typically scored overwhelming victories. In 1924, for instance, the team won by scores of 30–0, 22–0, 33–0, and 19–2 before beating the United States in the final 6–1, a relative nail-biter.

The first challenge to Canadian supremacy came in 1936. Great Britain suited up several top Canadian amateurs, claiming they were members of the British Commonwealth and therefore eligible to represent England in the competition. England beat Canada in the semifinals then played to a scoreless tie in triple-overtime against the U.S. to secure the gold. Canada regained its dominant position in the Olympics when the Games resumed after World War II, winning the gold in 1948 and 1952. In all, from 1920 to 1952, Canada lost just one Olympic hockey game.

In 1956, the Soviet Union entered a team in the competition for the first time. The sport had begun to take off in Russia, and because the top players were all employed in "other jobs" by the state, they technically were not professionals and thus eligible as amateurs. The Soviets played with great class and proficiency, winning all seven of their games to take the gold medal.

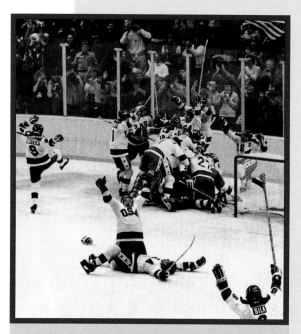

The impossible achieved: Team USA explodes into celebration after the final buzzer of their dramatic 4–3 victory over the heavily favored Soviets at the 1980 Winter Olympics in Lake Placid, New York.

This team was expected to repeat in 1960, with Canada rated as the top challenger, but the American team stunned the USSR in the semifinals to earn a shot at the gold. In the gold-medal game—which started the next morning at 8 A.M.—an emotionally and physically drained U.S. team found itself trailing Czechoslovakia 4–3 after two periods. Russian coach Nikolai Soloubov risked the ire of the Kremlin when he entered the American locker room and explained to the inexperienced players that all they needed was a little oxygen. A tank was located, the players sucked back some fresh air, and then scored six straight goals to win the gold medal. The Soviet Union reasserted itself in 1964, taking the gold in a tight final against Canada, then repeated as Olympic champion from 1968 to 1976.

In 1980 the United States brought a lightly regarded team to the Olympics; it featured nine members of the University of Minnesota's team and other players from various American colleges and amateur leagues. Coach Herb Brooks told his players (whose average age was 22) that if they trained fanatically hard they might be able to outskate some of the top teams and sneak into medal contention. They played together for 63 games before the Olympics, with moderate success, including a game against the Soviets. The Russian stars trounced Team USA 10-3 and barely broke a sweat.

When the 1980 Winter Olympics got under way in Lake Placid, New York, no one expected anything other than another gold-medal run from the Soviet Union. In the semifinal, the USSR was matched against Team USA, which to nearly everyone's surprise had snuck into the medal round, exhibiting a combination of hard work, heads-up play, and plain old dumb luck. As so often happens in the Olympics, the game was built up as a political battle, in this case matching the two superpowers of the Cold War against each other—and to the countrymen of each team, it was a war of good against evil.

Not even the most rabid American fans gave their team much of a chance, but this game was played on the ice. The Americans came out with a fury that caught the Soviets by surprise. Whenever a Russian player shot, an American sacrificed his body to stop it. Whenever a loose puck was up for grabs, the U.S. seemed to reach it first. And whenever the Russians let up, even for a second or two, an American player flew into the picture and capitalized on the opportunity. Team USA hung tough, trailing only 3–2 after two

The U.S. women's hockey team poses for the cameras after their gold-medal victory in the 1998 Winter Olympics. The two games they played against the powerful Canadian team were riveting, giving a great boost to women's hockey in its first Olympic appearance.

periods. Midway through the final stanza, the Americans scored two quick goals to take the lead. With the crowd on its feet chanting, *USA! USA! USA!* for the rest of the game, the unnerved Soviets failed to capitalize on one scoring opportunity after another. In a stirring conclusion, American bodies were flying all over the ice as U.S. goaltender Jim Craig withstood a 10-minute barrage without letting the puck in the net. When the final buzzer sounded, Team USA had pulled off a "Miracle on Ice." Even the Russians had to smile. Although on the losing end of a hard-fought game, they knew they had been part of a very special moment in their sport. The U.S. polished off Finland in the final to take a most improbable gold medal.

Sanity returned to the hockey world in 1984 when the Soviet Union won the gold and the U.S. failed to make the medal round. It was the same story in 1988, and again in 1992, when the Soviet squad competed and won as the Unified Team. The 1994 Olympics, held in Lillehammer, Norway, marked the end of Russian supremacy, as Sweden took the gold from Canada. The collapse of communism had gutted the Unified Team, as one star after another went for the big bucks and entered the National Hockey League. It was a situation that would have been unthinkable a decade earlier.

To Olympic purists, an even more unthinkable scenario developed for the 1998 Olympics in Nagano, Japan. For the first time, Olympic hockey competition was open to all players, including professionals. The National Hockey League interrupted its season so that its best players could rejoin their respective national teams and compete in Japan for a gold medal. There was a downside for the NHL, because when the Stanley Cup playoffs rolled around its top players would likely be pretty tired. But the league saw Nagano as a chance to market itself to a brand-new audience. Millions of people who do not watch hockey watch the Olympics, and the hope was that the ice-hockey competition would bring in new fans.

Hextall. The Canadiens won the Stanley Cup in 1986 behind the play of Mats Naslund and future superstars Chris Chelios and Patrick Roy. And the Calgary Flames reached the finals twice during the 1980s, winning the Cup in 1989.

With wide-open hockey being played throughout the league, offensive stars abounded. In Quebec, the Stastny brothers from Bratislava, Czechoslovakia, lifted a mediocre Nordiques team into playoff contenders. Anton and Marian played left and right wing, respectively, and combined for more than 400 points from 1981–82 to 1983–84. The star of the family was Peter, who centered for his brothers and averaged more than 100 points a season during his 10 seasons with the Nordiques. Quebec's best player was left wing Michel Goulet, who topped 40 goals seven years in a row during

The Canadian and U.S. teams were favored to meet in a gold-medal showdown, but it was the team from the Czech Republic that won. Unlike Team USA and Team Canada, the Czechs did not build their team completely with NHL stars. A core group of players was selected and trained in the Czech Republic for months before a handful of NHL stars—including Jaromir Jagr and Dominik Hasek—joined them for the final run. This proved to be the right combination, as the Czechs played cohesive, mistake-free hockey throughout the tournament and Jagr and Hasek came up huge when it counted. In the end, it was not the high-scoring NHL stars who dominated the tournament but the workmanlike play of the Czech defense that won the gold.

The really exciting story of the 1998 Olympics—at least for Americans—was the performance of the U.S. women's national team. Women's hockey was a medal sport for the first time at Nagano; only the most ardent U.S. fans even knew the team existed. But for several years, the U.S. had gained ground on the dominant Canadian team and by 1998 had, at the very least, pulled even. Still, the hockey experts were in shock when Canada lost the first-ever women's gold medal to the United States. After blitzing Canada 7–4 early in the tournament, Team USA played with the perfect blend of passion and patience when they met again in the tension-packed final. The result was a 3–1 victory. Although the women's team could hardly be characterized as an underdog, the final result of America's Olympic hockey experience was far from expected: The men's team returned without a medal, while the women were immortalized on a Wheaties box.

the 1980s. He used his lightning speed to blow past defenders—no fancy moves, no tricky stickhandling—and was particularly deadly on the power play, when he peppered opposing goalies with shots from every part of the offensive zone.

The Los Angeles Kings developed one of the best close-in players ever to take the ice in left wing Luc Robitaille. Robitaille's ability to read a play and skate to where the open shot was going to be put him in marvelous position to score goals. His lightning-quick release and deadly aim—especially up high and through the goalie's pads—enabled him to top 40 goals in each of his first eight seasons.

Denis Savard had the scoring touch, too. In 10 years with the Blackhawks, he topped 90 points seven times, and scored 40 or more goals 3 years in a row. The

THE HOCKEY NEWS

NHL ATTENDANCE

$1.50 64522 THE INTERNATIONAL HOCKEY WEEKLY FEBRUARY 17, 1984 Vol. 37, No. 20

Maloney
Shines
Brightest
At All-Star
Classic

—Page 7

Reinhart
Wows
Doctors
With
Recovery

—Page 20

One
Goal:
Reliving
Team USA
Miracle

—Page 6

HOWE
SWEET
IT IS...

RED WING ROOKIE
STEVE YZERMAN

GORDIE HOWE

Steve Yzerman, a cover story as a rookie center for the Red Wings in 1983–84, put up big numbers from the moment he arrived in the NHL. But long-suffering Detroit fans would have to wait until 1997 for Yzerman and company to end a 42-year Stanley Cup drought that stretched back to Gordie Howe's glory days.

most agile center of the 1980s behind Gretzky, he could change directions with a single stride or shift gears and streak past an unwary defender. A great wrist shot and a knack for tucking the puck into impossibly small openings made him a threat to score anywhere inside the blue line.

Another center with superb finesse was Dale Hawerchuk, who broke in with the Winnipeg Jets in 1981 at the tender age of 18. Even as a teenager he delighted fans

with his ability to thread difficult passes to teammates. But Hawerchuk was equally talented as a scorer, especially on deflections, where his marvelous hand-eye coordination helped him redirect slap shots past helpless goalies. He scored 45 times as a rookie and topped the 40-goal mark six times in his first seven seasons.

With all the goal scoring going on in the 1980s, it is hard to believe that any defensemen managed to distinguish themselves. But three stood out as terrific all-around players and team leaders. Rod Langway, who broke into the pros as a teenager in the WHA, spent a couple of years in Montreal before moving on to the Washington Capitals. There he became the finest player in franchise history. His focus was almost entirely defensive; he ruled the area in front of the net like few before or since. Langway stood 6'3" and weighed 220 pounds, yet he was quick and agile. He made a study of opposing forwards, learning their tendencies and abilities, so he was rarely caught off guard. He used his body intelligently, burying opponents with hard checks but rarely taking a bad penalty. Langway was also a master at turning a play around and starting a break with a sharp pass up ice.

Chris Chelios, the first U.S.-born player to win the Norris Trophy, broke in with the Montreal Canadiens in the mid-1980s and was a key contributor to the team's 1986 championship. In the years following, he became one of the top defenders ever to take the ice and continued to star right through the 1990s with the Chicago Blackhawks. Chelios blended splendid hockey skills with fearsome intimidation, punishing the top scorers for opposing teams and clobbering anyone who so much as breathed on one of his teammates. Whether clearing a

SUPER MARIO

Had the 1980s not been a decade-long highlight show for Wayne Gretzky, they would have belonged to Mario Lemieux. Lemieux was a vision become real, the kind of extraordinary natural athlete that hockey fans had long suspected would someday arrive in the NHL. Lemieux, who first donned his Pittsburgh Penguins sweater in 1984, was the most astounding physical specimen ever to play hockey. He stood 6'4" and weighed 225 pounds, yet he moved with the speed, grace, and agility of a man 50 pounds lighter. Lemieux had a shot so strong and accurate that he could shoot at parts of the net that goalies simply assumed they had covered. His long arms and great stickwork made it impossible to strip the puck, but defenders could not just lay back when Lemieux crossed the blue line or he would throw them a fake and accelerate past them. Checking him was futile, and even taking a penalty on purpose did not always work, as he could easily drag a man on his back while tucking the puck past a helpless goaltender.

When Lemieux was not scoring, he was using his great vision to find open teammates. Either way he was a cinch to pick up at least one or two points a game; he finished his career averaging just a shade over two per contest. By the age of 22, Lemieux was the most feared player in hockey. He scored 70 goals and registered 98 assists to win the NHL scoring title in 1987–88, then followed that season with an even better one, with 199 points on 85 goals and 114 assists. As the 1980s drew to a close, Lemieux had taken the hapless Penguins—who in two decades had never won more than 40 games—to the verge of respectability. As the 1990s began, the Stanley Cup was up for grabs, and Super Mario aimed to bring it to Pittsburgh.

Huge and tremendously athletic, Mario Lemieux was a fearsomely talented hockey player. He stepped out from behind Wayne Gretzky's shadow late in the 1980s, winning four scoring titles and three MVP awards and carrying the Pittsburgh Penguins to two Stanley Cups.

center out of the slot or digging for loose pucks along the board, Chelios rarely lost a battle. No defenseman pressured the puck better when confronted with a fleet-footed forward.

The best defender of the period, however, was Ray Bourque of the Boston Bruins. Bourque carried on the team tradition of great defensemen by winning five Norris Trophies and making the first-team All-Star list a dozen times after breaking in with the Bruins in 1979. He did everything well from the moment he entered the NHL—he could read plays coming at him, and he could sense when to join the attack after play turned the other way. His skating, passing, and stickhandling were exceptional, and he almost never made a mistake with the puck. Bourque could do the dirty work his position demanded, but he could also deliver a lovely pass to a teammate for an easy goal. And although he played most of his career outside the Stanley Cup spotlight, he racked up more All-Star selections than any player besides Gordie Howe.

A Formula for Success

The mark of a great hockey player is his ability to make his teammates better. Ultimately, however, a player's greatness is judged by whether he has won a Stanley Cup. That might have been fair during the NHL's six-team era, when a truly great player could carry his team to the championship. But as the league expanded and the playoffs went from two rounds to four, the odds of any player—great or otherwise—winning a Stanley Cup became increasingly remote. When Mario Lemieux joined the

Pittsburgh Penguins in the mid-1980s, the team was so bad and fan interest so low that the local indoor soccer club was actually outdrawing the Penguins. Lemieux was expected to bring the franchise back from the dead, and this he did almost immediately. But it was a mighty long way from respectability to a Stanley Cup. Indeed, many Penguin fans merely assumed that Lemieux would become the best player never to win a championship.

This did not mean that Pittsburgh was not going to try. Management felt that if Lemieux could be surrounded with a few good young players and a couple of veterans, he might carry the team on his shoulders and win the Stanley Cup. In retrospect, it was a rather naive plan. No team had ever relied so heavily on one player to bring home a championship—not even the Oilers, who had Wayne Gretzky, the best player ever. But the Penguins recognized before anyone else that hockey was changing. Escalating salaries and free agency meant that teams could no longer keep the same organizations together year after year. The easiest players to cut loose were solid but unspectacular veterans and star players who had failed to blend into a particular team's style of play. This meant that the kind of talent the Penguins needed for their grand plan would become available from time to time.

Slowly but surely, they assembled just the team they needed to survive four rounds of postseason play. And in doing so, the Penguins established a how-to pattern for a decade of Stanley Cup champions. Pittsburgh needed a player who could trigger scoring opportunities from the defensive zone, so its first investment was in veteran Paul Coffey, whom the Oilers allowed to leave via free agency. The Pens picked up

Czech-born Jaromir Jagr's long reach and creative stickhandling are two of the elements that make him the NHL's most dangerous one-on-one player.

goalie Tom Barrasso from the Sabres, figuring he was on the verge of becoming a playoff-caliber player. Barrasso had jumped from high school to the NHL a few years earlier and won the Vezina Trophy, so they knew he could handle the pressure. Prior to the 1990–91 season, the Penguins lured former Islander Brian Trottier out of retirement, giving the team a trio of top-flight centers. They also grabbed right wing Joe Mullen, whose Stanley Cup experience with the Calgary Flames would prove invaluable. Meanwhile, left wing Kevin Stevens and right wing Mark Recchi developed into All-Stars, and early in 1991, the Penguins picked up playmaking defenseman Larry Murphy. The final piece of the puzzle was Czech sensation Jaromir Jagr, one of the most dazzling rookies to hit the league in years.

In 1990–91, the Penguins battled their way to the top of the tough Patrick Division, doing it without Lemieux, who missed two-thirds of the season with a bad back. Recchi had a great year, leading the team with 40 goals and 73 assists, and five other players netted 20 or more goals. In preparation for the playoffs, the team made an important trade with the Hartford Whalers. They acquired veteran center Ron Francis, one of the smartest and most talented support players in history. They also got a pair of enforcers—Ulf Samuelsson and Grant Jennings—to keep teams from roughing up Lemieux, who returned in time for the post-season.

The plan worked to perfection as Pittsburgh outlasted a pesky New Jersey Devils team and then cruised to easy wins over Washington and Boston to make the finals. After falling behind 2–1 to the Minnesota North Stars, the Penguins stormed back to take the final three games for the first Stanley Cup in franchise history. Lemieux, who scored 44 points in 23 games, won the Conn Smythe Trophy as playoff MVP.

In 1991–92, the Penguins went into battle with essentially the same team, except that Lemieux managed to play in all but 20 regular season games. A big change, however, did occur behind the bench—coach Bob Johnson died of cancer. Scotty Bowman was brought in to provide a steady hand during an unsteady time, and the players responded by finishing a difficult season healthy and focused. After surviving close calls against the Capitals and Rangers, Super Mario and company wiped out the Boston Bruins in the conference finals and blew the Chicago Blackhawks out of the rink in four straight to win the Cup. Lemieux was awarded the Conn Smythe Trophy again, becoming the first nongoalie to win it in back-to-back years.

The success of the Penguins set the tone for the rest of the 1990s. Other teams collected young talent from Canada, the United States, and Europe; went after experienced big-game performers; then added spare parts during the season to craft a team capable of going all the way. This formula worked for the Canadiens in 1993, the Rangers in 1994, the Devils in 1995, the Colorado Avalanche in 1996, and the Red Wings in 1997. Gone were the days when a franchise could nurse its young players along and slowly work them in with the veterans. As salaries and ticket prices soared,

fans demanded that their teams go into the playoffs with guns blazing. Any franchise appearing timid in this respect was crucified.

Montreal, whose heart-stopping march to the 1993 Stanley Cup included 10 overtime victories in 11 tries, followed the formula to perfection. The team's three top scorers were all picked up from other clubs after 1990. Each was a left wing who complemented existing players perfectly, giving the Canadiens three lines that could put the puck in the net. Vincent Damphousse had played with Toronto and Edmonton, Kirk Muller had been a standout for the Devils,

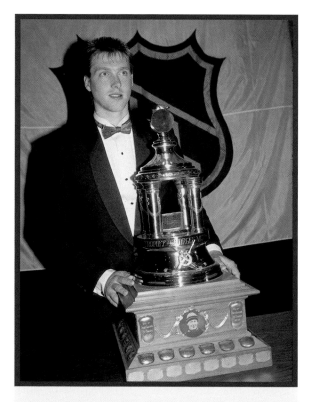

Patrick Roy, who has backstopped both the Canadiens and the Avalanche to Stanley Cups, receives the first of his three Vezina Trophies.

and Brian Bellows had spent a decade with Minnesota before a trade brought him to Montreal a couple of weeks before training camp opened in 1992. The Canadiens also had center Denis Savard, who was acquired from the Blackhawks two seasons earlier, and bruiser Rob Ramage, picked up from the Tampa Bay Lightning with fewer than a dozen games remaining in the regular season. The homegrown talent included centers John LeClair and Stephan Lebeau, right wing Mike Keane, and defenseman Mathieu Schneider.

Holding this team together was its innovative goaltender, Patrick Roy. He had earned his spurs back in 1986 when he helped the Canadiens win the Cup as a 21-year-old rookie. Now a veteran, he had perfected moves that other goalies never dreamed of and delighted in trash-talking opponents to distraction. Roy devised a modified butterfly style that required him to crouch with his pads just off the ice in an inverted V-shape. From this stance he could flop down and block a low shot or pop up to handle a high one. By the time he led the Canadiens to the 1993 Cup, Roy was a hero of such magnitude that thousands of little boys across Canada were tossing aside their sticks, grabbing pads and masks, and exploring life between the pipes.

Erasing The Curse

The New York Rangers were the next team to patch a squad together for the playoffs. Jeers of "1940!...1940!...1940!"—the last time the team took home a Stanley Cup—rained down on the Rangers whenever they took the ice in an enemy arena; long-suffering New York fans demanded a contender. The Ranger front office's first

move was to land a leader, and they found one in Mark Messier, whose goal-scoring output had dropped to 12 during an injury-riddled 1990–91 season with the Oilers. Acquiring Messier turned out to be a brilliant move—he still had great hockey left in him, and by the end of the Rangers' run to the Cup many were calling him the greatest team leader in the history of sport.

Over the next three seasons, the Rangers kept adding spare parts until the team was

An exultant Mark Messier holds aloft the Cup that Rangers fans had waited 54 years to see again. Messier's commanding presence and inspirational play during the Rangers' 1994 playoff run had many calling him the greatest leader in the history of team sports.

almost completely transformed. Messier had a big say in which players the Rangers went after, which is how former Oiler defensemen Kevin Lowe and Jeff Beukeboom and forwards Esa Tikkanen, Glenn Anderson and Craig MacTavish ended up on the team. Messier also had a say in who the Rangers got rid of; it was at his insistence that they dumped Tony Amonte and Mike Gartner. Adding an interesting twist to the lineup was a quartet of Russian imports—Alexei Kovalev, Sergei Zubov, Sergei Nemchinov, and Alexander Karpovtsev. New York's reliance on players with international résumés would be copied by successful teams throughout the decade.

By the time the 1994 playoffs rolled around the only offensive player still left from the fall of 1991 was Adam Graves, whom the Rangers had signed off the Edmonton roster a month before Messier came to town. The team's only home-grown talent was on defense and in goal. Two Americans, Brian Leetch and Mike Richter, teamed with Messier to give the Rangers as formidable a crease-to-crease threesome as there was in the league. Leetch established himself as New York's top player after winning the Calder Trophy in 1989 and blossomed into a superstar in 1991–92 when he collected 80 assists and won the Norris Trophy as the league's top defenseman. He was a coach's dream: quick feet, soft hands, an eye for an open man, and the ability to deliver accurate passes off the forehand or backhand. Working the point on the Ranger attack, Leetch kept the puck in the zone as well as anyone in the league, and his remarkable first step enabled him to zoom in on goal whenever the ice opened up. On defense, his lateral movement let him jam up opposing forwards as well as steal passes that other defensemen could not touch.

Behind Leetch's heroics, Richter provided clutch network. Darting back and forth between the pipes, the agile 185-pounder took the corners away from opposing shooters and handled rebounds and one-timers as well as anyone in the league. Richter's concentration and puck-stopping instincts gave the Rangers confidence that they could afford to make a couple of mistakes and not pay the price. In the spring of 1994, he was as sharp as he had ever been.

Throughout the postseason Messier, Leetch, and Richter performed brilliantly, rising to the occasion time after time. The Rangers disposed of the Islanders and Capitals in nine games before becoming locked in a death struggle with the defensive wizards across the Hudson River, the New Jersey Devils. The two clubs traded blows for four games, then the Devils came into Madison Square Garden and won to grab a 3–2 series lead. With the Rangers facing elimination in Game Six, Messier—who had become something more than human in the eyes of both fans and his teammates—guaranteed a victory, and then went onto New Jersey's home ice and tallied a natural hat trick in a dramatic come-from-behind 4–2 victory. Game Seven went into double overtime before veteran Stephane Matteau—picked up in a late-season trade with Chicago for Tony Amonte—ended it with a wraparound goal past Martin Brodeur.

In the finals, New York jumped out to a 3–1 lead, but the Vancouver Canucks came storming back to force a seventh game. In that contest, Leetch opened the scoring and Messier finished it as the Rangers edged the scrappy Canucks 3–2. At long last, Messier and his mates had ended the longest Stanley Cup drought in NHL history.

Devilish Defense

The 1994–95 season featured a lengthy labor dispute during which a total of 468 games were canceled. The schedule did not get under way until late in January. In the amended 48-game season, the Quebec Nordiques and Detroit Red Wings emerged as the NHL's new powerhouses. According to the experts, the fast-skating teams would have the advantage in the postseason, for they would be fresher than at the end of an 82-game campaign. But no one figured on the Devils, who used a tricky neutral zone trap that coach Jacques Lemaire borrowed from his old Montreal teams. Time and again, New Jersey's opponents were thwarted as they attempted to launch attacks up the ice, and as their frustration grew, they began to take unwise risks and turn the puck over at center ice. The Devil forwards turned these mistakes into easy scores, as New Jersey advanced to the Stanley Cup Finals with shocking ease.

There they met the Red Wings, who seemed to be too smart, too powerful, and too fast—even for the cagey Devils. But behind the inspired play of veterans Neal Broten and Claude Lemieux, New Jersey hung tough and capitalized on their few opportunities to win the first two games of the series on Detroit's home ice. Infused with confidence, the Devils proceeded to take the final two games from the bewildered Red Wings and complete the most improbable sweep in the history of the Stanley Cup Finals.

The Devils triumphed without so much as one household name in their lineup. Broten, who played for the 1980 U.S. Olympic team, tallied 4 game-winning goals, while Lemieux—known more for his fistwork than stickwork—scored 13 goals to win the Conn Smythe Trophy. The team's best offensive player, Stephane Richer, had never even scored 75 points as a Devil and was barely a factor against Detroit. Defenseman Scott Stevens, a valuable veteran acquired from the Blues, scored just once in the postseason. The only player who carved out any kind of reputation during the 1995 playoffs was goalie Martin Brodeur. In only his second full season, he exhibited the coolness under pressure that usually takes years to develop. He allowed no garbage goals, and made good saves when he had to; his concentration was not shattered by the pucks that did manage to get past him. Not that there were that many—he allowed a stingy 1.67 goals per game during the playoffs, recording three shutouts in 20 games. A boyhood fan of Patrick Roy, Brodeur distinguished himself as the dominant young goalie on the NHL scene with his ability to adjust his style to suit any team, shooter, or situation.

Avalanche in Colorado

After failing to win the Stanley Cup in 1995, the Red Wings were nearly run out of town. The Quebec Nordiques were the other favorite to win that year's Cup, but after their season ended with a playoff loss to the Rangers, they actually *did* leave town. The Nordiques, usually a mediocre club, were for once stocked with talent. Penny-pinching owner Marcel Aubut felt he needed the increased revenues that come with a new arena to be able to pay his players what they were worth. When the

Swedish native Peter Forsberg has been a key component of the powerful Colorado Avalanche teams of recent years.

government turned down Aubut's request, he found himself with little choice other than to sell the team.

In Denver, a company called Ascent Entertainment had been angling to acquire an expansion franchise from the NHL. When the Nordiques became available, the company switched tactics and jumped at the chance to buy the team. Thus, the up-and-coming Quebec Nordiques became the Colorado Avalanche.

The Avalanche had a fine core of players to start the 1995–96 season. Center Joe Sakic was one of the classiest players in the league, establishing himself as a solid 100-point man and a peerless leader. Always a good passer, he became a strong and accurate shooter in 1995. Coupled with an explosive first step, Sakic's improved offensive arsenal created all sorts of opportunities for linemates. Left wing Valeri Kamensky, a speedy Russian import with a

quick, deadly shot, was one of the most feared open-ice players in the game. He worked especially well with linemate Peter Forsberg, who at 22 was on the verge of becoming the team's most potent offensive player in just his second NHL season. Right up there with Sakic as a playmaker, the Swedish native reminded many of Wayne Gretzky in the way he saw plays unfolding before him. But at 6 feet and 190 pounds, he had the muscle that enabled him to crash through defenders and create opportunities when nothing was there. He and Sakic combined for 236 points in 1995–96.

Forsberg had been the key acquisition in a 1992 trade with the Philadelphia Flyers that saved the Nordiques from taking up permanent residence in the NHL's outhouse. Winners of just 12 games in 1990–91, the Nordiques got the first pick in the draft, which they used to select Eric Lindros. The 18-year-old junior-hockey legend was the most coveted youngster ever to come into the NHL. Many scouts said he could have been a productive pro at the age of 16. But Lindros, an intelligent and sensitive young man, felt that it was unfair for him to have to start his career with the league's worst team. After a year of intense negotiation, Marcel Aubut decided that he should entertain offers for Lindros. Had the holdout lasted any longer, he might have ended up with nothing. Or worse, Lindros might have sued the league and brought about an end to the draft. The Philadelphia Flyers made the winning bid, and they sent a package of draft picks and players to Quebec, as well as a large sum of cash.

While Lindros whipped the Flyers back into contention, the Quebec franchise used the money to keep its best players while continuing to wheel and deal to put together a championship team. From the players received in exchange for Lindros, the Avalanche eventually ended up with Forsberg, workhorse center Adam Deadmarsh, hard-hitting left wing Chris Simon, right wing Mike Keane, defenseman Uwe Krupp, center Mike Ricci, and the man who proved to be the icing on the cake: Patrick Roy. After nearly 300 wins in a Canadien uniform, the all-time great had a falling out with Montreal coach Mario Tremblay and was unceremoniously shipped to the Avalanche in December 1995.

Furious at his banishment, Roy vowed to lead Colorado to the Stanley Cup. And that is just what he did. He finished the season 22–15–1 for the Avalanche and simply dominated in the playoffs, winning 16 games and recording a 2.10 goals-against average. He was terrific against the Winnipeg Jets, Chicago Blackhawks, and heavily favored Detroit Red Wings, then completely shut down the Florida Panthers, who had advanced to the finals with a Devils-like combination of tough defense and clutch goaltending. In the end, the Avalanche simply overwhelmed its rivals in the playoffs. While Roy shut down the opposition, Sakic, Forsberg, and Kamensky scored 38 goals in 22 games and defensemen Krupp and Ozolinsh combined for 35 points.

Double Cups for Detroit

The Red Wings finally fulfilled their destiny in the spring of 1997. Ironically, their victory came just when their fans had given up hope of ever seeing another Stanley Cup. The team went into the postseason with just 38 wins as compared with 63 the previous year, and the goaltending situation was anything but clear. Although no one took the Wings lightly, the team that had won 25 more games in 1996 seemed far more imposing than the 1997 model. But this was a different Detroit squad in ways that did not necessarily show up in the victory column.

A few games into the 1996–97 season, Detroit management sent a message to its players by trading Stanley Cup specialist Paul Coffey, rising star Keith Primeau, and a number one draft choice to the Whalers for left wing Brendan Shanahan. The Red Wings lacked a player who could step up and lead the team during the playoffs, and they felt that the 28-year-old sharpshooter could assume this role. The deal served as a wakeup call for Steve Yzerman, who had been Detroit's star of stars and team captain for more than a decade. Yzerman's father had raised him to play hard and keep his mouth shut, but after 13 spectacular seasons and 500 goals he was viewed by many as a player who could not get it done when it really counted.

Almost overnight Stevie Wonder transformed himself into a gritty, vocal player and seized control of the Red Wings both in the locker room and on the ice. Yzerman's leadership proved to be the missing ingredient for Detroit, which already had a core of talented championship-caliber players—including five veterans of CSKA Moscow, one of the world's great teams during the 1980s and early 1990s. Viacheslav Fetisov, Igor Larionov, and Vladimir Konstantinov had more than 50 years of combined service in the hockey wars, while centers Vyacheslav Kozlov and Sergei Fedorov were just hitting their prime years. Fetisov, the 1994 Hart Trophy winner, ranked among the finest two-way players ever to take the ice.

Another key contributor was Swedish import Nicklas Lidstrom, a solid defenseman whose emerging offensive skills made Coffey expendable. Just prior to the playoffs the team began to fuse into a cohesive unit. Former Penguin defenseman Larry Murphy was added to the roster with a dozen games to go, and Stanley Cup veteran Mike Vernon stepped in for young Chris Osgood as the Red Wing goalie.

In the playoffs, Detroit disposed of the Blues and Mighty Ducks to set the stage for a revenge match with the Avalanche in the Western Conference final. This time the Red Wings dictated play, and Vernon outdueled Roy to give his team a six-game victory and a berth in the Stanley Cup Finals opposite the Philadelphia Flyers. The series was over almost before it got started, as the Red Wings played the kind of smart, inspired hockey that had been missing in Detroit since the 1950s. The Flyers dropped a pair of tough games in their own building, then got blown out in Game Three when the series returned to Detroit. The fourth and final game was decided on a magnificent goal by Detroit's Darren McCarty, the team's fearless and underrated right wing. Like so many of the Detroit players, he found his niche just as the season concluded, becoming a key factor throughout the playoffs, especially against the Avalanche.

Detroit's prospects for another Stanley Cup in 1998 began to look slim only six days after capturing the 1997 Cup. The Wings were to gather for one final team meeting before splitting up for the summer, but three club members—Viacheslav Fetisov, Vladimir Konstantinov, and team masseur Sergei Mnatsakanov—never made it. The limousine carrying them to the meet-

ing crashed, leaving Mnatsakanov partially paralyzed and Konstantinov, in many ways the heart and soul of the team, the victim of brain damage. Fetisov sustained relatively minor injuries and would be ready to take the ice by training camp, but another key member of the 1997 team, goaltender Mike Vernon, had taken the free-agent route out of Detroit. And star center Sergei Fedorov would hold out in a contract dispute with management for most of the year. As the season progressed few gave the Red Wings, with their aging, slow-footed defense and often-erratic goalkeeping, a chance to repeat—in the East, New Jersey and Philadelphia seemed poised to become the true powerhouses, and in the West the Colorado Avalanche and Dallas Stars (formerly the Minnesota North Stars) were scoring in bunches.

The Red Wings, however, believed. They had dedicated their season to their fallen comrades Konstantinov and Mnatsakanov. As the playoffs got under way, the teams most likely to wrest the Cup from the Wings sputtered. New Jersey, Philadelphia, and Colorado all went down in shocking first-round upsets, and though Dallas survived an opening-round series against the San Jose Sharks, they lost their top scorer, Joe Nieuwendyk, to an injury. The Red Wings, meanwhile, relied on their depth to fight past first the Phoenix Coyotes and then the St. Louis Blues, setting up a showdown in the conference finals against their division rival Dallas. Without Nieuwendyk, the Stars could not match Detroit's scoring output and the Wings blew by them in six games.

Meanwhile, the early exits of the top-ranked teams in the East led to an unlikely conference final matching the Buffalo

Sabres, led by Vezina and Hart Trophy–winning goalie Dominik Hasek, against the Washington Capitals, who had ridden a hot netminder of their own through the first two rounds of the playoffs. Olaf Kolzig may actually have been better than Hasek in the first two rounds of the playoffs, and he sustained his effort against the Sabres; with Kolzig walling off the goal and some clutch overtime scoring, the Capitals took the series 4–2 and advanced to the Stanley Cup Finals for the first time in team history.

In the Cup Finals, the Red Wings were not to be denied. They swept the Caps 4–0, and after the final victory Yzerman handed the Cup to wheelchair-bound Vladimir Konstantinov. In a moment that instantly became one of the emotional highlights in team-sports history, Konstantinov, only a year ago one of the top defensemen in hockey, held the Cup aloft as his teammates pushed him around the ice.

Vancouver's John McIlhargey (right) and New York's Nick Fotiu (dubbed Early Man by the Ranger faithful), two players whose fists kept them in the league for years, square off in a 1977 game. Intimidation and goons have always been a part of hockey's culture and remain so, though the NHL has made some attempts to clean up the game.

The Globalization of Hockey

John LeClair's emergence as a high-scoring star put him in an elite class of American players that had been growing steadily since the mid-1980s. This group included forwards Keith Tkachuk, Jeremy Roenick, Mike Modano, and Pat LaFontaine; defensemen Brian Leetch, Chris Chelios, Derian Hatcher, and Brian Berard; and goalies Mike Richter and John Vanbiesbrouck. These players led Team USA to the World Cup in 1996, establishing the United States as a first-class hockey power. Despite the national squad's disappointing showing in the 1998 Olympics, when the Winter Games come to Salt Lake City in 2002,

Team USA should take the ice as a favorite to make the gold medal final.

This will likely depend on the development of youngsters such as Tkachuk and Berard, who began their NHL careers with woeful franchises but quickly established themselves among the dominant young players at their positions. Tkachuk, the lone superstar with the Jets during their final seasons in Winnipeg, blossomed into the league's top goal scorer when the franchise moved to Phoenix and became the Coyotes in 1996. A powerful left wing who relishes the opportunity to throw his weight around, he became only the second player in history

LINDROS AND THE LEGION OF DOOM

The second half of the 1990s was an era of unfulfilled promise for the Philadelphia Flyers. Loaded with young talent, the Flyers seemed to be a lock to win a Cup, but the team fell short in the playoffs each year from 1995 to 1998. The Flyers' key player as the millennium neared was Eric Lindros. After coming into the league touted as the prototype for hockey's next generation, Eric Lindros used his size, skill, and intelligence to succeed the old-fashioned way: by making his teammates better. John LeClair, a serviceable left wing with the Canadiens, blossomed into a 50-goal scorer when he joined Philadel-phia in a 1995 trade. With Lindros tying up defenders in the slot or along the boards, LeClair found himself free to power his way to the goal one on one. Mikael Renberg, a capable two-way player when he came to the Flyers from Sweden in 1993, became one of the league's best all-around right wings. Lin-dros's dominance in the offensive end en-abled Renberg to contribute goals and assists without overcommitting himself,

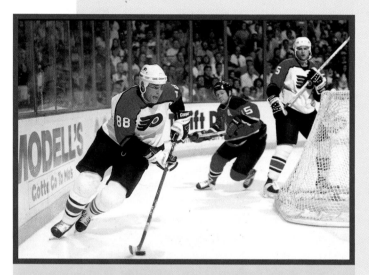

Eric Lindros came into the NHL touted as a can't-miss superstar. Though a dominant force in the league, he has yet to carry the Flyers back to Stanley Cup glory.

and thus he became a valuable defensive component. Lindros, LeClair, and Renberg—each a big, aggressive skater—became known as the Legion of Doom, but the im-pact of Lindros was felt throughout the Flyer lineup. Even defenseman Janne

to tally 50 goals and rack up 200 penalty minutes in the same season. In another era, Tkachuk would have been a gung-ho middle linebacker in the NFL. This is sig-nificant, for as the 21st century looms ahead, it appears that many of the young American athletes who might have auto-matically pursued football careers in the past are now being drawn to hockey.

Berard could be an important figure in this evolution, too. When he was acquired by the Islanders in a 1996 trade with the Ottawa Senators, New York fans immedi-ately began predicting that he would be-come the next Denis Potvin. Berard fulfilled these expectations by winning the Calder Trophy as a 19-year-old with some very Potvin-like end-to-end play. Tradition has

Niinimaa, a rookie from Finland, became a tiger on the power play in 1997 thanks to the havoc created by Lindros when Philly had a man advantage.

Lindros himself improved each year, learning how to intimidate without throwing his body all over the ice. He also developed his finesse game to a point at which he could dart around an opponent instead of barreling over him. And the soft hands and great balance that so impressed observers when he was in the juniors only improved as he reached his prime in the NHL.

But Lindros, perhaps unfairly considering how young he still was, would have to endure seeing his leadership abilities questioned after the Flyers' annual playoff failures. In 1995, Lindros's third season in the league, the Flyers jumped from mediocrity to the Atlantic Division title, but they were knocked out of the playoffs by the Devils. In 1996, the Florida Panthers, in only their third NHL season, dumped the heavily favored Flyers from the second round behind the stingy goaltending of John Vanbiesbrouck.

Lindros became truly dominant in 1997, and with the midseason pickup of Paul Coffey from the Whalers and the presence of veteran centers Dale Hawerchuk and Rob Brind'Amour, Philadelphia looked like a juggernaut going into the playoffs. In what seemed like a scripted Stanley Cup playoff run, the Flyers beat the Penguins and Rangers on their way to the finals, with Pittsburgh's Lemieux and New York's Gretzky seeming to pass the torch to Lindros. But everything went shockingly wrong against Detroit. The Red Wings, whose overall depth was too much for Philadelphia, swept by the Flyers in four straight. It was more of the same in 1998, with the Flyers going down in the first round at the hands of the Buffalo Sabres. The Flyers could manage only one victory against Sabre goalie Dominik Hasek, with both Lindros and LeClair performing poorly. Philadelphia fans can only hope that the pain of defeat will push Lindros to take his extraordinary skills to a championship level.

long been a cornerstone of hockey's appeal, and even in these turbulent times of strikes, contract squabbles, and free agency, fans still believe that a team's players are linked to one another down through time. For Berard, a Rhode Island native, to be considered worthy of carrying on Potvin's good name is a heartening development for hockey in the United States. No longer are U.S. players dismissed out of hand. One day, perhaps, an American player may even find enough elbow room between Richard, Howe, Gretzky, and Lemieux to be considered one of the greatest ever.

Of course, he would first have to distinguish himself from the current crop of Canadian-born superstars, not to mention the growing legion of top players from overseas. Besides Detroit's Russian Connection, other stars from the former Soviet Union to distinguish themselves in the 1990s included Pavel Bure, Alexander Mogilny, Alexei Yashin, and Peter Bondra. And Sandis Ozolinsh, from Latvia, became one of the NHL's top defensemen. Finland produced a pair of top performers with scoring machine Teemu Selanne—who shattered the rookie mark for goals with 76—and Saku Koivu, an exceptional playmaking center. All-Star Peter Forsberg headed a strong group of Swedish forwards including big, powerful Mats Sundin and Daniel Alfredsson, whose combination of hustle and shooting branded him as one of the league's up-and-coming young talents.

The country that generated the most impressive burst of talent was the Czech Republic. Zigmund Palffy, Petr Nedved, and Josef Stumpel—while not among the NHL's most gifted players—had carved out reputations as smart, intuitive performers who maximized their strengths and worked hard to improve on their weaknesses. Jaromir Jagr and Dominik Hasek oozed with talent from the day they hit the league; they combined their skills with intelligence and creativity to become perhaps the league's two most dynamic performers of the late 1990s. Jagr, who joined the Penguins in time to win two Stanley Cups, learned the pro game playing beside Mario Lemieux. He not only proved the perfect winger for the all-time great center, but when Lemieux sat out the 1994–95 season while undergoing radiation therapy for Hodgkin's disease, Jagr stepped up and led the NHL in scoring. The following year, with Super Mario back in action, Jagr netted 62 goals and delivered 87 assists to fin-

ish with 149 points—the most ever by a right wing. Jagr's skating skills left opponents in awe from the day he came to the NHL. Defensemen learned quickly that trying to shadow him was foolish, and his good balance meant that he could not be muscled off the puck. During the 1990s, Jagr developed an arsenal of moves and shots that made him the most dangerous offensive player in the league, and no player has ever taken the ice night after night with as much sheer joy as Jagr.

Dominik Hasek, who was stuck behind Ed Belfour in the Chicago Blackhawk system, blossomed after a 1992 trade to the Buffalo Sabres. He won his first of three Vezina Trophies in 1993–94, becoming the first netminder to turn in a sub-2.00 goals-against average in two decades. In 1996–97, Hasek won the Hart Trophy, becoming the first goalie to earn MVP honors in 35 years. A five-time goalie of the year in his home country, Hasek came to the NHL at 25 with an intriguing combination of horrible technique and spellbinding reflexes. His technique did not improve much, but he made believers out of even his harshest critics by stopping more pucks than anyone in the game. Hasek sprawled, flailed, kicked, dove, and did whatever else he could to make a save, but he never appeared to be anything other than in full control. Supremely confident, he felt he could save any shot he could see, often shouting for his defensemen to clear out of the way. In his world, goalies win games. And no one in recent times has done more to keep his team on top than Hasek, as witnessed by his remarkable performances against the Canadian and Russian national teams during the Czech Republic's gold-medal run at the 1998 Olympics.

The elastic and supremely confident Dominik Hasek has been the NHL's best goaltender in the late 1990s.

With so many talented Americans and Europeans in the NHL, the stakes became much higher for pro hockey's Canadian-born talent. This was especially true for defensemen, who now had to be fast skaters and good stickhandlers as well as being big and tough. In the late 1990s, the old guard of Canadian backliners—Paul Coffey, Ray Bourque, Larry Murphy, Al MacInnis, and Scott Stevens—gave way to a new generation of defensive stars, almost all of whom hailed from the U.S. and Europe. At the forward position, however, Canadian-raised talent still reigned supreme as the NHL approached the millennium; at least half of the league's top centers and wingers were born

in Canada. Among the most notable were right wing Brett Hull and left wing Paul Kariya.

Hull, the son of all-time great Bobby Hull, broke in with the Calgary Flames in the late 1980s and blossomed into a prolific goal scorer after a trade to the St. Louis Blues. From 1990 to 1992, he scored 228 goals, leading the league each year. Living up to his Hall of Famer dad was not easy—Hull was not as fast and did not shoot as hard as his father, and he was often criticized for his chunky frame and lax attitude toward practice. But over the years he worked hard and improved his play in all three zones and even developed an accurate passing touch. At a stage in his career when other players begin to beg off the ice, he upped his minutes to around 30 a game. As good as his other skills became, though, it was Hull's ability to put the puck in the net that kept his name in the headlines. In the blink of an eye, he could take a skittering puck and one-time it toward the goal with tremendous speed and accuracy. Defensemen had no chance to block Hull's quick shot, and goalies could only hope they had

time to flick out a pad or stick and deflect it. Comparisons to Hall of Famer Mike Bossy were not without merit, although the two players in many ways were quite different. But it is hardly a coincidence that the only right wing to score his 500th career goal faster than Hull was the old Islander sharpshooter.

Paul Kariya, who broke in with the Anaheim Mighty Ducks in 1994, worked hard to live up to the example of his boyhood

Brett Hull has parlayed a blazing slap shot and the instincts and accuracy of a sniper into a Hall of Fame career rivaling that of his father, Bobby Hull.

idol, Wayne Gretzky. Similar in size and skating ability, Kariya quickly became one of the league's most dangerous offensive performers, and he had perfected many of the Great One's moves in only his second season. That year saw Kariya blossom into a creative one-on-one player who could combine speed, intelligence, stickhandling, and shooting to strike fear into the hearts of defensemen throughout the NHL. Fans loved to watch him work his way down the ice, passing the puck to himself off the boards, skating circles around opponents, and torturing goalies by swooping around the crease and behind the net. In an era when 50-goal scorers were fast disappearing, Kariya established himself as a threat to score 50 a season well into the next decade.

The Future

If Paul Kariya is the future of the NHL, then fans should get their money's worth every night. He is smart, strong, and quick and seems to cherish every minute he spends on the ice. He may also be symbolic of the changes in store for hockey, as he embodies many of the emerging trends in the game. A native of British Columbia, Kariya was reared in a culture steeped in Canada's rich hockey tradition, yet he was also exposed to other influences through his father, who was born in Japan and became a member of the national rugby team after emigrating to Canada. During a stellar career in the juniors, Kariya played summer lacrosse, a sport that requires players to shoot with either hand. After graduating from high school, he accepted a scholarship to the University of Maine, where he won the Hobey Baker Award as the NCAA's top player in

his freshman year. During his sophomore year, Kariya also appeared for Team Canada during the Olympics and the World Cup. By the time he hit the NHL, the young man had more international experience and a broader athletic background than the majority of veterans in the league. He even became an accomplished juggler when he read that it helped coordinate both sides of the brain.

Not every young NHL player is as multifaceted as Paul Kariya, of course, nor as talented. But the coming generation of professional hockey players is infinitely more sophisticated and highly trained than the generation that produced the genius of Wayne Gretzky and Mario Lemieux. Who is to say what the next century will bring in terms of the quality and caliber of play. Athletes will no doubt be bigger, stronger, and faster, and that will have a profound impact on the speed and force with which hockey is played. The NHL in recent years has become much more aggressive in promoting itself and has poured a lot of resources into promoting hockey at a grassroots level, especially in the United States.

It has long been said that the difference between Canadian and American hockey players is that in Canada kids learn to skate as soon as they can walk and that controlling a puck with a stick is practically second nature. Though clearly an exaggeration, there is considerable truth in the idea that the vast majority of young athletes in the U.S. have limited exposure to hockey, or no exposure at all. With the explosion in the growth of roller hockey and the expansion of the NHL into the Sunbelt, an opportunity exists to put skates on the feet and sticks in the hands of millions of kids who might never have considered a hockey career.

What might such exposure bring? The possibilities are intriguing. Think of the phenomenal athletes who today just miss making it in other pro sports: the rock-hard six-foot point guard who is too short to make it in the NBA, or the 6'5" outside linebacker who is a tenth of a second too slow in the 40-yard dash to make the grade in the NFL. Had they been playing hockey their whole lives instead of basketball or football, they might be millionaire hockey players today. And the game would be very, very different if enough athletes like this were available. If hockey continues to grow in the U.S., the day when an NHL squad looks more like an NFL squad might not be too far off. Of course, the great thing about hockey is that no matter how big and strong the average player becomes, there is always room for the little guy to survive and thrive.

A Hockey Timeline

1885 The first true hockey league is formed in Kingston, Ontario. Queen's University, the Royal Military College, the Kingston Hockey Club, and Kingston Athletics compete, with Queen's winning the championship; the five-team Amateur Hockey Association of Canada is formed; ice strength is limited to seven skaters per side.

1893 The Montreal Amateur Athletic Association team is awarded the first Stanley Cup.

1894 The Montreal AAAs defeat the Ottawa Capitals in the first Stanley Cup defense.

1898 The Montreal Victorias successfully defend the Stanley Cup for the third time.

1899 The AHA disbands, but league officials start the Canadian Amateur Hockey League.

1904 Michigan dentist Doc Gibson forms the International Pro Hockey League.

1905 Frank McGee of the Ottawa Silver Seven scores 14 goals against Dawson City in one Stanley Cup game.

1906 The Ottawa Silver Seven successfully defend the Stanley Cup for the 10th straight time.

1908 The Ontario Professional Hockey League—Canada's first true pro circuit—is formed.

1909 The National Hockey Association—forerunner of the NHL—is formed.

1910 Thirty-minute halves are replaced by three 20-minute periods.

1911 The NHA reduces the number of skaters from seven to six.

1912 The Pacific Coast Hockey Association begins play in January.

1915 The Vancouver Millionaires become the first PCHA team to win the Stanley Cup.

1917 The Seattle Metropolitans become the first U.S. club to win the Stanley Cup; the NHA suspends operations; and the National Hockey League is organized on November 22 in Montreal; the first NHL game is played on December 19; goalies are permitted to leave their feet to make saves.

1918 The Stanley Cup Finals are extended from five to seven games; blue lines are added to the rink; assists are officially counted for the first time; Joe Malone of the Montreal Canadiens scores 44 goals in 20 games.

1920 Joe Malone scores a record seven goals in a game.

1921 Minor penalties are reduced from three minutes to two; the Western Canadian Hockey League is formed as a rival to the PCHA.

1922 Punch Broadbent of the Ottawa Senators scores a goal in 25 consecutive games; the NHL abandons its split-season format and its top two teams play for the right to take on the winner of the PCHA-WCHL playoff for the Stanley Cup.

1923 Clint Benedict of the Senators leads the league in goals-against average for the fifth consecutive season; the first NHL game is broadcast on radio.

1924 Canada wins the first Olympic hockey gold medal; Cy Denneny of the Ottawa Senators wins the scoring title despite recording just one assist; Boston is granted the NHL's first U.S. franchise.

1925 Lester Patrick leads Victoria to the Stanley Cup, marking the last time a West Coast team would win the trophy; Frank Nighbor of the Senators wins the first Lady Byng Trophy for gentlemanly play; the New York Americans are granted an NHL franchise.

1926 The New York Rangers, Chicago Blackhawks, and Detroit Cougars join the league; the NHL is split into Canadian and American Divisions; the Toronto St. Patricks change their name to the Maple Leafs.

1927 The NHL gets control of the Stanley Cup after the demise of western pro hockey; the Canadiens donate the Vezina Trophy.

1928 Howie Morenz of the Canadiens, playing in 43 games, becomes the first NHL player to reach the 50-point plateau; 45-year-old coach Lester Patrick fills in for his injured goalie and spurs his New York Rangers to a Stanley Cup championship.

1929 George Hainsworth of the Canadiens sets a record with 22 shutouts; forward passing is allowed in the attacking zone for the first time the following season, and goal scoring soars.

1930 The forerunner of the current offsides rule is adopted; the Detroit Cougars become the Falcons; the first four-sided electronic clocks appear in NHL arenas.

1932 The Falcons become the Red Wings.

1934 The first All-Star Game is played as a benefit for injured star Ace Bailey; the modern penalty-shot rule is adopted.

1935 Charlie Conacher of the Maple Leafs becomes the first back-to-back scoring champ in NHL history.

1936 The Canadiens finish with the league's worst record. The NHL, hoping to rebuild its key franchise, gives Montreal first refusal on all French-Canadian players for three years.

1937 The league adopts an early form of the icing rule.

1938 The second All-Star Game is played to benefit the family of the late Howie Morenz; Eddie Shore wins the Hart Trophy for the fourth time in six seasons; the Chicago Blackhawks suit up eight American-born players and win the Stanley Cup.

1940 Boston's Kraut Line of Milt Schmidt, Woody Dumart, and Bob Bauer finish 1-2-3 in NHL scoring; Red Horner of the Maple Leafs leads the league in penalty minutes for the eighth year in a row.

1942 The Maple Leafs erase a 0–3 deficit in the finals to win the Stanley Cup; the Americans withdraw from the league, leaving six teams; wartime restrictions on train travel lead to the elimination of overtime.

1943 NHL president Frank Calder dies. The league commissions the Calder Cup, to be awarded to the NHL's outstanding rookie.

1944 Maurice Richard becomes the NHL's first 50-goal scorer, while teammate Elmer Lach is the first player to top 50 assists.

1945 Philadelphia, Los Angeles, and San Francisco apply for NHL franchises but are later turned down by the league.

1946 Clarence Campbell succeeds Merv Dutton as NHL president.

1947 The All-Star Game becomes an annual event.

1948 The NCAA holds its first championship tournament.

1950 Pete Babando of the Red Wings scores an overtime goal in Game Seven of the finals to give Detroit the Stanley Cup; the first NHL draft is held.

1951 Gordie Howe leads the league in scoring for the first of four straight years.

1952 Canada wins its last Olympic gold medal; the Red Wings win the Stanley Cup without dropping a single game in the playoffs.

1953 The AHL Cleveland Barons— whose application for a league franchise is turned down—challenge the NHL champs for the Stanley Cup. The NHL refuses.

1954 The Norris Trophy is awarded to the league's top defenseman.

1956 The University of Michigan wins its fifth NCAA title in six years; the potency of the Montreal power play leads to a rule allowing a penalized skater to return to the ice when a goal is scored.

1957 Maurice Richard scores his 500th career goal.

1960 The Americans win the gold medal at the Squaw Valley Olympics; Jacques Plante of the Canadiens leads the league in goals-against average for the fifth straight season.

1961 Bernie Geoffrion becomes history's second 50-goal scorer; the Hockey Hall of Fame opens in Toronto.

1962 Gordie Howe scores his 500th career goal; Bobby Hull scores 50 goals for the Blackhawks.

1965 For the first time, the Conn Smythe Trophy is awarded to the most outstanding player in the postseason.

1967 The California Seals, Los Angeles Kings, Minnesota North Stars, Pittsburgh Penguins, and St. Louis Blues join the NHL, ending the Six-Team Era.

1969 The amateur draft is expanded to cover any player in the world; Phil Esposito becomes the first player to top 100 points in a season.

1970 Bobby Hull scores his 500th career goal; Bobby Orr becomes the first defenseman to top 100 points in a season; the Buffalo Sabres and Vancouver Canucks join the league.

1971 Jean Beliveau scores his 500th career goal; Esposito sets a new single-season record with 76 goals; Orr is the first player to amass 100 assists in a season.

1972 Orr becomes the first player to win the Hart Trophy three years in a row; Team Canada defeats the USSR in a dramatic preseason series; the Atlanta Flames and New York Islanders join the NHL; the World Hockey Association begins operations and signs Bobby Hull.

1973 Frank Mahovlich scores his 500th career goal; the Hartford Whalers win the first AVCO Cup as WHA champions; the United States Hockey Hall of Fame is opened; Gordie Howe and sons Marty and Mark take the ice together for the WHA Houston Aeros.

1974 Esposito wins his fourth straight scoring title; goalie Bernie Parent of the Flyers wins a record 47 games; 47-year-old Gordie Howe wins the WHA MVP award and leads the Aeros to the AVCO Cup; the Washington Capitals and Kansas City Scouts join the NHL.

1975 Dave Schultz of the Flyers sets a record with 472 penalty minutes; Bobby Hull sets a new pro record with 77 goals and leads the WHA Winnipeg Jets to the AVCO Cup.

1976 Darryl Sittler of the Maple Leafs tallies 10 points in one game; for the first time, four players reach the 50-goal plateau in the same season; Reggie Leach of the Flyers scores a record 19 goals during the playoffs; the Seals move to Cleveland and are renamed the Barons; the Scouts move to Colorado and are renamed the Rockies.

1977 John Ziegler succeeds Clarence Campbell as NHL president.

1978 A record 11 Boston Bruins finish the season with 20 or more goals; Swedish stars Anders Hedberg and Ulf Nilsson team with Bobby Hull to lead the Jets to the WHA championship. The Barons and North Stars merge.

1979 Seventeen-year-old Wayne Gretzky finishes third in the WHA scoring race during the league's final season; four new teams join the NHL after the WHA folds: the Edmonton Oilers, Hartford Whalers, Quebec Nordiques, and Winnipeg Jets; all players entering the NHL are forced to wear

helmets—veterans are allowed to choose whether they want to wear them.

1980 Wayne Gretzky scores 51 goals and ties for the scoring lead in his first NHL season; Team USA upsets the USSR on its way to a dramatic gold-medal victory in Lake Placid; the Flames move to Calgary.

1982 Gretzky tops the 200-point mark for the first time in league history and sets a record with 92 goals; the Rockies move to New Jersey and become the Devils.

1983 Overtime returns to the regular season.

1984 Dale Hawerchuk of the Jets records a record five assists in one period; Gretzky gets a record 10 hat tricks for the second time in his career and tallies a goal or assist in 51 straight games.

1986 Gretzky tops the 200-point mark for the third year in a row, with a record 215; Tim Kerr of the Flyers scores a record 34 power play goals; Paul Coffey of the Oilers sets a record for defensemen with 48 goals.

1987 Gretzky wins the Hart Trophy for the seventh year in a row.

1988 The Soviet Union wins its seventh gold medal; Mario Lemieux becomes the first player to beat Gretzky in the scoring race since 1979.

1989 Lemieux becomes the second player to tally more than 100 assists in a season.

1991 Theoren Fleury of the Flames scores three shorthanded goals in a game; Brett Hull of the Blues sets a record for right wings with 86 goals; the San Jose Sharks join the league; the shape of the crease is changed from a box to a semicircle; video replays are used to assist referees.

1992 The Unified Team wins the gold medal at the Albertville Olympics; the players strike for the first time, holding up play for 11 days in April; the Ottawa Senators and Tampa Bay Lightning join the league.

1993 Luc Robitaille of the Kings sets a record for left wings with 63 goals; Teemu Selanne sets a record for rookies with 76 goals; a record 14 players score 50 or more goals; the Montreal Canadiens win their 24th Stanley Cup—the most championships ever for a major-league sports franchise; Gary Bettman is named NHL commissioner; the Anaheim Mighty Ducks and Florida Panthers join the league; the North Stars move to Dallas and become the Stars.

1994 Gretzky surpasses Gordie Howe for the all-time NHL goal-scoring record; the Rangers win their first Stanley Cup in 54 years; Russia's Sergei Federov becomes the first overseas player to win the Hart Trophy; a labor dispute in the fall leads to the cancellation of 468 games; Sweden wins the gold medal at the Lillehammer Olympics.

1995 Play resumes after dispute is settled, with 48-game schedule; the Nordiques move to Colorado and are renamed the Avalanche.

1996 Grant Fuhr of the Blues sets a record for goalies by playing in 79 straight games; Joe Sakic scores six game-winning goals in the playoffs and leads the Avalanche to the Stanley Cup; the Winnipeg Jets move to Phoenix and are renamed the Coyotes.

1997 The Whalers move to North Carolina and become the Hurricanes; the Red Wings win their first Stanley Cup since 1955; 17-year-old Joe Thornton of the Bruins is the youngest number-one draft choice in league history.

1998 Dominik Hasek leads the Czech Republic to the gold medal at the Nagano Olympics. The competition marks the first time NHL players are allowed to compete in the games. Hasek becomes the first goalie to win back-to-back Hart Trophies. For the first time since 1970, only one player—Jaromir Jagr—finishes a full season with more than 100 points.

Appendix A
Stanley Cup Champions

Season	Champion
1893	Montreal AAAs*
1894	Montreal AAAs
1895	Montreal Victorias*
1896	Montreal Victorias & Winnipeg Victorias
1897	Montreal Victorias
1898	Montreal Victorias*
1899	Montreal Shamrocks
1900	Montreal Shamrocks
1901	Winnipeg Victorias
1902	Montreal AAAs
1903	Ottawa Silver Seven
1904	Ottawa Silver Seven
1905	Ottawa Silver Seven
1906	Montreal Wanderers
1907	Montreal Wanderers & Kenora Thistles
1908	Montreal Wanderers
1909	Ottawa Senators*
1910	Montreal Wanderers
1911	Ottawa Senators
1912	Quebec Bulldogs
1913	Quebec Bulldogs
1914	Toronto Blueshirts
1915	Vancouver Millionaires
1916	Montreal Canadiens
1917	Seattle Metropolitans
1918	Toronto Arenas
1919	Montreal Canadiens & Seattle Metropolitans**
1920	Ottawa Senators
1921	Ottawa Senators
1922	Toronto St. Pats
1923	Ottawa Senators
1924	Montreal Canadiens
1925	Victoria Cougars
1926	Montreal Maroons
1927	Ottawa Senators
1928	New York Rangers
1929	Boston Bruins
1930	Montreal Canadiens
1931	Montreal Canadiens
1932	Toronto Maple Leafs
1933	New York Rangers
1934	Chicago Blackhawks
1935	Montreal Maroons
1936	Detroit Red Wings
1937	Detroit Red Wings
1938	Chicago Blackhawks
1939	Boston Bruins
1940	New York Rangers
1941	Boston Bruins
1942	Toronto Maple Leafs
1943	Detroit Red Wings
1944	Montreal Canadiens
1945	Toronto Maple Leafs
1946	Montreal Canadiens
1947	Toronto Maple Leafs
1948	Toronto Maple Leafs
1949	Toronto Maple Leafs
1950	Detroit Red Wings
1951	Toronto Maple Leafs
1952	Detroit Red Wings
1953	Montreal Canadiens
1954	Detroit Red Wings
1955	Detroit Red Wings
1956	Montreal Canadiens
1957	Montreal Canadiens
1958	Montreal Canadiens
1959	Montreal Canadiens
1960	Montreal Canadiens
1961	Chicago Blackhawks
1962	Toronto Maple Leafs
1963	Toronto Maple Leafs
1964	Toronto Maple Leafs
1965	Montreal Canadiens
1966	Montreal Canadiens
1967	Toronto Maple Leafs
1968	Montreal Canadiens
1969	Montreal Canadiens
1970	Boston Bruins
1971	Montreal Canadiens
1972	Boston Bruins

1973	Montreal Canadiens	1988	Edmonton Oilers
1974	Philadelphia Flyers	1989	Calgary Flames
1975	Philadelphia Flyers	1990	Edmonton Oilers
1976	Montreal Canadiens	1991	Pittsburgh Penguins
1977	Montreal Canadiens	1992	Pittsburgh Penguins
1978	Montreal Canadiens	1993	Montreal Canadiens
1979	Montreal Canadiens	1994	New York Rangers
1980	New York Islanders	1995	New Jersey Devils
1981	New York Islanders	1996	Colorado Avalanche
1982	New York Islanders	1997	Detroit Red Wings
1983	New York Islanders	1998	Detroit Red Wings
1984	Edmonton Oilers		
1985	Edmonton Oilers		
1986	Montreal Canadiens		
1987	Edmonton Oilers		

* No challengers to Cup

** Flu epidemic caused cancellation of series after five games; each team had two wins and a tie

APPENDIX B
Annual Awards
Art Ross Trophy
(League Scoring Leader)

Year	Winner	Runner-Up
1918	Joe Malone, Montreal Canadiens	Cy Denneny, Ottawa
1919	Newsy Lalonde, Montreal Canadiens	Odie Cleghorn, Montreal Canadiens
1920	Joe Malone, Quebec	Newsy Lalonde, Montreal Canadiens
1921	Newsy Lalonde, Montreal Canadiens	Cy Denneny, Ottawa
1922	Punch Broadbent, Ottawa	Babe Dye, Toronto
1923	Babe Dye, Toronto	Billy Boucher, Montreal
1924	Cy Denneny, Ottawa	Babe Dye, Toronto
1925	Babe Dye, Toronto	Howie Morenz, Montreal Canadiens
1926	Nels Stewart, Montreal Maroons	Carson Cooper, Boston
1927	Bill Cook, New York Rangers	Dick Irvin, Chicago
1928	Howie Morenz, Montreal Canadiens	Aurel Joliat, Montreal Canadiens
1929	Ace Bailey, Toronto	Nels Stewart, Montreal Maroons
1930	Cooney Weiland, Boston	Frank Boucher, New York Rangers
1931	Howie Morenz, Montreal Canadiens	Ebbie Goodfellow, Detroit
1932	Harvey Jackson, Toronto	Joe Primeau, Toronto
1933	Bill Cook, New York Rangers	Harvey Jackson, Toronto
1934	Charlie Conacher, Toronto	Joe Primeau, Toronto
1935	Charlie Conacher, Toronto	Syd Howe, St. Louis–Detroit
1936	Dave Schriner, New York Americans	Marty Barry, Detroit

1937	Dave Schriner, New York Americans	Syl Apps, Toronto
1938	Gordie Drillon, Toronto	Syl Apps, Toronto
1939	Toe Blake, Montreal	Dave Schriner, New York Americans
1940	Milt Schmidt, Boston	Woody Dumart, Boston
1941	Bill Cowley, Boston	Bryan Hextall, New York Rangers
1942	Bryan Hextall, New York Rangers	Lynn Patrick, New York
1943	Doug Bentley, Chicago	Bill Cowley, Boston
1944	Herbie Cain, Boston	Doug Bentley, Chicago
1945	Elmer Lach, Montreal Canadiens	Maurice Richard, Montreal Canadiens
1946	Max Bentley, Chicago	Gaye Stewart, Toronto
1947	Max Bentley, Chicago	Maurice Richard, Montreal Canadiens
1948	Elmer Lach, Montreal Canadiens	Buddy O'Connor, New York Rangers
1949	Roy Conacher, Chicago	Doug Bentley, Chicago
1950	Ted Lindsay, Detroit	Sid Abel, Detroit
1951	Gordie Howe, Detroit	Maurice Richard, Montreal Canadiens
1952	Gordie Howe, Detroit	Ted Lindsay, Detroit
1953	Gordie Howe, Detroit	Ted Lindsay, Detroit
1954	Gordie Howe, Detroit	Maurice Richard, Montreal Canadiens
1955	Bernie Geoffrion, Montreal Canadiens	Maurice Richard, Montreal Canadiens
1956	Jean Beliveau, Montreal Canadiens	Gordie Howe, Detroit
1957	Gordie Howe, Detroit	Ted Lindsay, Detroit
1958	Dickie Moore, Montreal Canadiens	Henri Richard, Montreal Canadiens
1959	Dickie Moore, Montreal Canadiens	Jean Beliveau, Montreal Canadiens
1960	Bobby Hull, Chicago	Bronco Horvath, Boston
1961	Bernie Geoffrion, Montreal Canadiens	Jean Beliveau, Montreal Canadiens
1962	Bobby Hull, Chicago	Andy Bathgate, New York Rangers
1963	Gordie Howe, Detroit	Andy Bathgate, New York Rangers
1964	Stan Mikita, Chicago	Bobby Hull, Chicago
1965	Stan Mikita, Chicago	Norm Ullman, Detroit
1966	Bobby Hull, Chicago	Stan Mikita, Chicago
1967	Stan Mikita, Chicago	Bobby Hull, Chicago
1968	Stan Mikita, Chicago	Phil Esposito, Boston
1969	Phil Esposito, Boston	Bobby Hull, Chicago
1970	Bobby Orr, Boston	Phil Esposito, Boston
1971	Phil Esposito, Boston	Bobby Orr, Boston
1972	Phil Esposito, Boston	Bobby Orr, Boston
1973	Phil Esposito, Boston	Bobby Clarke, Philadelphia
1974	Phil Esposito, Boston	Bobby Orr, Boston
1975	Bobby Orr, Boston	Phil Esposito, Boston
1976	Guy Lafleur, Montreal Canadiens	Bobby Clarke, Philadelphia
1977	Guy Lafleur, Montreal Canadiens	Marcel Dionne, Los Angeles
1978	Guy Lafleur, Montreal Canadiens	Bryan Trottier, New York Islanders
1979	Bryan Trottier, New York Islanders	Marcel Dionne, Los Angeles
1980	Marcel Dionne, Los Angeles	Wayne Gretzky, Edmonton
1981	Wayne Gretzky, Edmonton	Marcel Dionne, Los Angeles

1982	Wayne Gretzky, Edmonton	Mike Bossy, New York Islanders
1983	Wayne Gretzky, Edmonton	Peter Stastny, Quebec
1984	Wayne Gretzky, Edmonton	Paul Coffey, Edmonton
1985	Wayne Gretzky, Edmonton	Jari Kurri, Edmonton
1986	Wayne Gretzky, Edmonton	Mario Lemieux, Pittsburgh
1987	Wayne Gretzky, Edmonton	Jari Kurri, Edmonton
1988	Mario Lemieux, Pittsburgh	Wayne Gretzky, Edmonton
1989	Mario Lemieux, Pittsburgh	Wayne Gretzky, Los Angeles
1990	Wayne Gretzky, Los Angeles	Mark Messier, Edmonton
1991	Wayne Gretzky, Los Angeles	Brett Hull, St. Louis
1992	Mario Lemieux, Pittsburgh	Kevin Stevens, Pittsburgh
1993	Mario Lemieux, Pittsburgh	Pat Lafontaine, Buffalo
1994	Wayne Gretzky, Los Angeles	Sergei Fedorov, Detroit
1995	Jaromir Jagr, Pittsburgh	Eric Lindros, Philadelphia
1996	Mario Lemieux, Pittsburgh	Jaromir Jagr, Pittsburgh
1997	Mario Lemieux, Pittsburgh	Teemu Selanne, Anaheim

Hart Trophy
(League MVP)

Year	Winner	Runner-up
1924	Frank Nighbor, Ottawa	Sprague Cleghorn, Montreal Canadiens
1925	Billy Burch, Hamilton	Howie Morenz, Montreal Canadiens
1926	Nels Stewart, Montreal Maroons	Sprague Cleghorn, Boston
1927	Herb Gardiner, Montreal Canadiens	Bill Cook, New York Rangers
1928	Howie Morenz, Montreal Canadiens	Roy Worters, Pittsburgh
1929	Roy Worters, New York Americans	Ace Bailey, Toronto
1930	Nels Stewart, Montreal Maroons	Lionel Hitchman, Boston
1931	Howie Morenz, Montreal Canadiens	Eddie Shore, Boston
1932	Howie Morenz, Montreal Canadiens	Joe Primeau, Toronto
1933	Eddie Shore, Boston	Bill Cook, New York Rangers
1934	Aurel Joliat, Montreal Canadiens	Lionel Conacher, Chicago
1935	Eddie Shore, Boston	Charlie Conacher, Toronto
1936	Eddie Shore, Boston	Hooley Smith, Montreal Maroons
1937	Babe Siebert, Montreal Canadiens	Lionel Conacher, Montreal Maroons
1938	Eddie Shore, Boston	Paul Thompson, Chicago
1939	Toe Blake, Montreal Canadiens	Syl Apps, Toronto
1940	Ebbie Goodfellow, Detroit	Syl Apps, Toronto
1941	Bill Cowley, Boston	Dit Clapper, Boston
1942	Tom Anderson, Brooklyn	Syl Apps, Toronto
1943	Bill Cowley, Boston	Doug Bentley, Chicago
1944	Babe Pratt, Toronto	Bill Cowley, Boston
1945	Elmer Lach, Montreal Canadiens	Maurice Richard, Montreal Canadiens

1946	Max Bentley, Chicago	Gaye Stewart, Toronto
1947	Maurice Richard, Montreal Canadiens	Milt Schmidt, Boston
1948	Buddy O'Connor, New York Rangers	Frank Brimsek, Boston
1949	Sid Abel, Detroit	Bill Durnan, Montreal Canadiens
1950	Charlie Rayner, New York Rangers	Ted Kennedy, Toronto
1951	Milt Schmidt, Boston	Maurice Richard, Montreal Canadiens
1952	Gordie Howe, Detroit	Elmer Lach, Montreal Canadiens
1953	Gordie Howe, Detroit	Al Rollins, Chicago
1954	Al Rollins, Chicago	Red Kelly, Detroit
1955	Ted Kennedy, Toronto	Harry Lumley, Toronto
1956	Jean Beliveau, Montreal Canadiens	Tod Sloan, Toronto
1957	Gordie Howe, Detroit	Jean Beliveau, Montreal Canadiens
1958	Gordie Howe, Detroit	Andy Bathgate, New York Rangers
1959	Andy Bathgate, New York Rangers	Gordie Howe, Detroit
1960	Gordie Howe, Detroit	Bobby Hull, Chicago
1961	Bernie Geoffrion, Montreal Canadiens	Johnny Bower, Toronto
1962	Jacques Plante, Montreal Canadiens	Doug Harvey, New York Rangers
1963	Gordie Howe, Detroit	Stan Mikita, Chicago
1964	Jean Beliveau, Montreal Canadiens	Bobby Hull, Chicago
1965	Bobby Hull, Chicago	Norm Ullman, Detroit
1966	Bobby Hull, Chicago	Jean Beliveau, Montreal Canadiens
1967	Stan Mikita, Chicago	Ed Giacomin, New York Rangers
1968	Stan Mikita, Chicago	Jean Beliveau, Montreal Canadiens
1969	Phil Esposito, Boston	Jean Beliveau, Montreal Canadiens
1970	Bobby Orr, Boston	Tony Esposito, Chicago
1971	Bobby Orr, Boston	Phil Esposito, Boston
1972	Bobby Orr, Boston	Ken Dryden, Montreal Canadiens
1973	Bobby Clarke, Philadelphia	Phil Esposito, Boston
1974	Phil Esposito, Boston	Bernie Parent, Philadelphia
1975	Bobby Clarke, Philadelphia	Rogatien Vachon, Los Angeles
1976	Bobby Clarke, Philadelphia	Denis Potvin, New York Islanders
1977	Guy Lafleur, Montreal Canadiens	Bobby Clarke, Philadelphia
1978	Guy Lafleur, Montreal Canadiens	Bryan Trottier, New York Islanders
1979	Bryan Trottier, New York Islanders	Guy Lafleur, Montreal Canadiens
1980	Wayne Gretzky, Edmonton	Marcel Dionne, Los Angeles
1981	Wayne Gretzky, Edmonton	Mike Liut, St. Louis
1982	Wayne Gretzky, Edmonton	Bryan Trottier, New York Islanders
1983	Wayne Gretzky, Edmonton	Pete Peeters, Boston
1984	Wayne Gretzky, Edmonton	Rod Langway, Washington
1985	Wayne Gretzky, Edmonton	Dale Hawerchuk, Winnipeg
1986	Wayne Gretzky, Edmonton	Mario Lemieux, Pittsburgh
1987	Wayne Gretzky, Edmonton	Ray Bourque, Boston
1988	Mario Lemieux, Pittsburgh	Grant Fuhr, Edmonton
1989	Wayne Gretzky, Los Angeles	Mario Lemieux, Pittsburgh
1990	Mark Messier, Edmonton	Ray Bourque, Boston

1991	Brett Hull, St. Louis	Wayne Gretzky, Los Angeles
1992	Mark Messier, New York Rangers	Patrick Roy, Montreal Canadiens
1993	Mario Lemieux, Pittsburgh	Doug Gilmour, Toronto
1994	Sergei Fedorov, Detroit	Dominik Hasek, Buffalo
1995	Eric Lindros, Philadelphia	Jaromir Jagr, Pittsburgh
1996	Mario Lemieux, Pittsburgh	Mark Messier, New York Rangers
1997	Dominik Hasek, Buffalo	Paul Kariya, Anaheim

Norris Trophy
(Top Defenseman)

Year	Winner	Runner-up
1954	Red Kelly, Detroit	Doug Harvey, Montreal Canadiens
1955	Doug Harvey, Montreal Canadiens	Red Kelly, Detroit
1956	Doug Harvey, Montreal Canadiens	Bill Gadsby, New York Rangers
1957	Doug Harvey, Montreal Canadiens	Red Kelly, Detroit
1958	Doug Harvey, Montreal Canadiens	Bill Gadsby, New York Rangers
1959	Tom Johnson, Montreal Canadiens	Bill Gadsby, New York Rangers
1960	Doug Harvey, Montreal Canadiens	Allan Stanley, Toronto
1961	Doug Harvey, Montreal Canadiens	Marcel Pronovost, Detroit
1962	Doug Harvey, New York Rangers	Pierre Pilote, Chicago
1963	Pierre Pilote, Chicago	Carl Brewer, Toronto
1964	Pierre Pilote, Chicago	Tim Horton, Toronto
1965	Pierre Pilote, Chicago	Jacques Laperriere, Montreal Canadiens
1966	Jacques Laperriere, Montreal Canadiens	Pierre Pilote, Chicago
1967	Harry Howell, New York Rangers	Pierre Pilote, Chicago
1968	Bobby Orr, Boston	J.C. Tremblay, Montreal Canadiens
1969	Bobby Orr, Boston	Tim Horton, Toronto
1970	Bobby Orr, Boston	Brad Park, New York Rangers
1971	Bobby Orr, Boston	Brad Park, New York Rangers
1972	Bobby Orr, Boston	Brad Park, New York Rangers
1973	Bobby Orr, Boston	Guy Lapointe, Montreal Canadiens
1974	Bobby Orr, Boston	Brad Park, New York Rangers
1975	Bobby Orr, Boston	Denis Potvin, New York Islanders
1976	Denis Potvin, New York Islanders	Brad Park, New York Rangers-Boston
1977	Larry Robinson, Montreal Canadiens	Borje Salming, Toronto
1978	Denis Potvin, New York Islanders	Brad Park, Boston
1979	Denis Potvin, New York Islanders	Larry Robinson, Montreal Canadiens
1980	Larry Robinson, Montreal Canadiens	Borje Salming, Toronto
1981	Randy Carlyle, Pittsburgh	Denis Potvin, New York Islanders
1982	Doug Wilson, Chicago	Ray Bourque, Boston
1983	Rod Langway, Washington	Mark Howe, Philadelphia
1984	Rod Langway, Washington	Paul Coffey, Edmonton

1985	Paul Coffey, Edmonton	Ray Bourque, Boston
1986	Paul Coffey, Edmonton	Mark Howe, Philadelphia
1987	Ray Bourque, Boston	Mark Howe, Philadelphia
1988	Ray Bourque, Boston	Scott Stevens, Washington
1989	Chris Chelios, Montreal Canadiens	Paul Coffey, Pittsburgh
1990	Ray Bourque, Boston	Al MacInnis, Calgary
1991	Ray Bourque, Boston	Al MacInnis, Calgary
1992	Brian Leetch, New York Rangers	Ray Bourque, Boston
1993	Chris Chelios, Chicago	Ray Bourque, Boston
1994	Ray Bourque, Boston	Scott Stevens, New Jersey
1995	Paul Coffey, Detroit	Chris Chelios, Chicago
1996	Chris Chelios, Chicago	Ray Bourque, Boston
1997	Brian Leetch, New York Rangers	Vladimir Konstantinov, Detroit

Vezina Trophy
(Top Goalie)

Year	Winner	Runner-up
1927	George Hainsworth, Montreal Canadiens	Clint Benedict, Mont. Maroons
1928	George Hainsworth, Montreal Canadiens	Alex Connell, Ottawa
1929	George Hainsworth, Montreal Canadiens	Tiny Thompson, Boston
1930	Tiny Thompson, Boston	Charlie Gardiner, Chicago
1931	Roy Worters, New York Americans	Charlie Gardiner, Chicago
1932	Charlie Gardiner, Chicago	Alex Connell, Detroit
1933	Tiny Thompson, Boston	John Roach, Detroit
1934	Charlie Gardiner, Chicago	Wilf Cude, Detroit
1935	Lorne Chabot, Chicago	Alex Connell, Mont. Maroons
1936	Tiny Thompson, Boston	Mike Karakas, Chicago
1937	Normie Smith, Detroit	Dave Kerr, New York Rangers
1938	Tiny Thompson, Boston	Dave Kerr, New York Rangers
1939	Frank Brimsek, Boston	Dave Kerr, New York Rangers
1940	Dave Kerr, New York Rangers	Frank Brimsek, Boston
1941	Turk Broda, Toronto	Frank Brimsek, Boston (tie)
		Johnny Mowers, Detroit (tie)
1942	Frank Brimsek, Boston	Turk Broda, Toronto
1943	Johnny Mowers, Detroit	Turk Broda, Toronto
1944	Bill Durnan, Montreal Canadiens	Paul Bibeault, Toronto
1945	Bill Durnan, Montreal Canadiens	Harry Lumley, Detroit (tie)
		Frank McCool, Toronto (tie)
1946	Bill Durnan, Montreal Canadiens	Frank Brimsek, Boston
1947	Bill Durnan, Montreal Canadiens	Turk Broda, Toronto
1948	Turk Broda, Toronto	Harry Lumley, Detroit
1949	Bill Durnan, Montreal Canadiens	Harry Lumley, Detroit

1950	Bill Durnan, Montreal Canadiens	Harry Lumley, Detroit
1951	Al Rollins, Toronto	Terry Sawchuk, Detroit
1952	Terry Sawchuk, Detroit	Al Rollins, Toronto
1953	Terry Sawchuk, Detroit	Gerry McNeil, Montreal Canadiens
1954	Harry Lumley, Toronto	Terry Sawchuk, Detroit
1955	Terry Sawchuk, Detroit	Harry Lumley, Toronto
1956	Jacques Plante, Montreal Canadiens	Glenn Hall, Detroit
1957	Jacques Plante, Montreal Canadiens	Glenn Hall, Detroit
1958	Jacques Plante, Montreal Canadiens	Marcel Paille, New York Rangers (tie)
		Lorne Worsley, New York Rangers (tie)
1959	Jacques Plante, Montreal Canadiens	Johnny Bower, Toronto (tie)
		Ed Chadwick, Toronto (tie)
1960	Jacques Plante, Montreal Canadiens	Glenn Hall, Chicago
1961	Johnny Bower, Toronto	Glenn Hall, Chicago
1962	Jacques Plante, Montreal Canadiens	Johnny Bower, Toronto
1963	Glenn Hall, Chicago	Johnny Bower, Toronto (tie)
		Don Simmons, Toronto (tie)
1964	Charlie Hodge, Montreal Canadiens	Glenn Hall, Chicago
1965	Johnny Bower, Toronto (tie)	Roger Crozier, Detroit
	Terry Sawchuk, Toronto (tie)	
1966	Charlie Hodge, Montreal (tie)	Glenn Hall, Chicago
	Lorne Worsley, Montreal (tie)	
1967	Denis Dejordy, Chicago (tie)	Charlie Hodge, Montreal Canadiens
	Glenn Hall, Chicago (tie)	
1968	Rogatien Vachon, Montreal (tie)	Johnny Bower, Toronto (tie)
	Lorne Worsley, Montreal (tie)	Bruce Gamble, Toronto (tie)
1969	Glenn Hall, St. Louis (tie)	Ed Giacomin, New York Rangers
	Jacques Plante, St. Louis (tie)	
1970	Tony Esposito, Chicago	Jacques Plante, St. Louis (tie)
		Ernie Wakely, St. Louis (tie)
1971	Ed Giacomin, New York Rangers (tie)	Tony Esposito, Chicago
	Gilles Villemure, New York Rangers (tie)	
1972	Tony Esposito, Chicago (tie)	Cesare Maniago, Minnesota (tie)
	Gary Smith, Chicago (tie)	Lorne Worsley, Minnesota (tie)
1973	Ken Dryden, Montreal Canadiens	Ed Giacomin, New York Rangers (tie)
		Gilles Villemure, New York Rangers (tie)
1974	Tony Esposito, Chicago (tie)	Gilles Gilbert, Boston
	Bernie Parent, Philadelphia (tie)	
1975	Bernie Parent, Philadelphia	Gary Edwards, Los Angeles (tie)
		Rogatien Vachon, Los Angeles (tie)
1976	Ken Dryden, Montreal Canadiens	Glenn Resch, New York Islanders
		Billy Smith, New York Islanders
1977	Ken Dryden, Montreal (tie)	Glenn Resch, New York Islanders (tie)
	Michel Larocque, Montreal (tie)	Billy Smith, New York Islanders (tie)
1978	Ken Dryden, Montreal (tie)	Bernie Parent, Philadelphia (tie)

	Michel Larocque, Montreal (tie)	Wayne Stephenson, Philadelphia (tie)
1979	Ken Dryden, Montreal (tie)	Glenn Resch, New York Islanders (tie)
	Michel Larocque, Montreal (tie)	Billy Smith, New York Islanders (tie)
1980	Don Edwards, Buffalo (tie)	Gerry Cheevers, Boston (tie)
	Bob Sauve, Buffalo (tie)	Gilles Gilbert, Boston (tie)
1981	Denis Herron, Montreal (tie)	Pete Peeters, Philadelphia (tie)
	Michel Larocque, Montreal (tie)	Rick St. Croix, Philadelphia (tie)
	Richard Sevigny, Montreal (tie)	
1982	Billy Smith, New York Islanders	Grant Fuhr, Edmonton
1983	Pete Peeters, Boston	Roland Melanson, New York Islanders
1984	Tom Barrasso, Buffalo	Rejean Lemelin, Calgary
1985	Pelle Lindbergh, Philadelphia	Tom Barrasso, Buffalo
1986	John Vanbiesbrouck, New York Rangers	Bob Froese, Philadelphia
1987	Ron Hextall, Philadelphia	Mike Liut, Hartford
1988	Grant Fuhr, Edmonton	Tom Barrasso, Buffalo
1989	Patrick Roy, Montreal Canadiens	Mike Vernon, Calgary
1990	Patrick Roy, Montreal Canadiens	Daren Puppa, Buffalo
1991	Ed Belfour, Chicago	Patrick Roy, Montreal Canadiens
1992	Patrick Roy, Montreal Canadiens	Kirk McLean, Vancouver
1993	Ed Belfour, Chicago	Tom Barrasso, Pittsburgh
1994	Dominik Hasek, Buffalo	John Vanbiesbrouck, Florida
1995	Dominik Hasek, Buffalo	Ed Belfour, Chicago
1996	Jim Carey, Washington	Chris Osgood, Detroit
1997	Dominik Hasek, Buffalo	Martin Brodeur, New Jersey

Calder Trophy
Rookie of the Year

Year	Winner	Runner-up
1933	Carl Voss, Detroit	
1934	Russ Blinko, Montreal Maroons	
1935	Dave Schriner, New York Americans	Bert Connolly, New York Rangers
1936	Mike Karakas, Chicago	Bucko McDonald, Detroit
1937	Syl Apps, Toronto	Gordie Drillon, Toronto
1938	Cully Dahlstrom, Chicago	Murph Chamberlain, Toronto
1939	Frank Brimsek, Boston	Roy Conacher, Boston
1940	Kilby MacDonald, New York Rangers	Wally Stanowski, Toronto
1941	Johnny Quilty, Montreal Canadiens	Johnny Mowers, Detroit
1942	Grant Warwick, New York Rangers	Buddy O'Connor, Montreal Canadiens
1943	Gaye Stewart, Toronto	Glen Harmon, Montreal Canadiens
1944	Gus Bodnar, Toronto	Bill Durnan, Montreal Canadiens
1945	Frank McCool, Toronto	Ken Smith, Boston
1946	Edgar Laprade, New York Rangers	George Gee, Chicago
1947	Howie Meeker, Toronto	Jimmy Conacher, Detroit

1948	Jim McFadden, Detroit	Pete Babando, Boston
1949	Pentti Lund, New York Rangers	Allan Stanley, New York Rangers
1950	Jack Gelineau, Boston	Phil Maloney, Boston
1951	Terry Sawchuk, Detroit	Al Rollins, Toronto
1952	Bernie Geoffrion, Montreal Canadiens	Hy Buller, New York Rangers
1953	Lorne Worsley, New York Rangers	Gordie Hannigan, Toronto
1954	Camille Henry, New York Rangers	Earl Reibel, Detroit
1955	Ed Litzenberger, Chicago	Don McKenney, Boston
1956	Glenn Hall, Detroit	Andy Hebenton, New York Rangers
1957	Larry Regan, Boston	Ed Chadwick, Toronto
1958	Frank Mahovlich, Toronto	Bobby Hull, Chicago
1959	Ralph Backstrom, Montreal Canadiens	Carl Brewer, Toronto
1960	Bill Hay, Chicago	Murray Oliver, Detroit
1961	Dave Keon, Toronto	Bob Nevin, Toronto
1962	Bobby Rousseau, Montreal Canadiens	Cliff Pennington, Boston
1963	Kent Douglas, Toronto	Doug Barkley, Detroit
1964	Jacques Laperriere, Montreal Canadiens	John Ferguson, Montreal Canadiens
1965	Roger Crozier, Detroit	Ron Ellis, Toronto
1966	Brit Selby, Toronto	Bert Marshall, Detroit
1967	Bobby Orr, Boston	Ed Van Impe, Chicago
1968	Derek Sanderson, Boston	Jacques Lemaire, Montreal Canadiens
1969	Danny Grant, Minnesota	Norm Ferguson, Oakland
1970	Tony Esposito, Chicago	Bill Fairbairn, New York Rangers
1971	Gilbert Perreault, Buffalo	Jude Drouin, Minnesota
1972	Ken Dryden, Montreal Canadiens	Rick Martin, Buffalo
1973	Steve Vickers, New York Rangers	Bill Barber, Philadelphia
1974	Denis Potvin, New York Islanders	Tom Lysiak, Atlanta
1975	Eric Vail, Atlanta	Pierre Larouche, Pittsburgh
1976	Bryan Trottier, New York Islanders	Glenn Resch, New York Islanders
1977	Willi Plett, Atlanta	Don Murdoch, New York Rangers
1978	Mike Bossy, New York Islanders	Barry Beck, Colorado
1979	Bobby Smith, Minnesota	Ryan Walter, Washington
1980	Ray Bourque, Boston	Mike Foligno, Detroit
1981	Peter Stastny, Quebec	Larry Murphy, Los Angeles
1982	Dale Hawerchuk, Winnipeg	Barry Pederson, Boston
1983	Steve Larmer, Chicago	Phil Housley, Buffalo
1984	Tom Barrasso, Buffalo	Steve Yzerman, Detroit
1985	Mario Lemieux, Pittsburgh	Chris Chelios, Montreal Canadiens
1986	Gary Suter, Calgary	Wendel Clark, Toronto
1987	Luc Robitaille, Los Angeles	Ron Hextall, Philadelphia
1988	Joe Nieuwendyk, Calgary	Ray Sheppard, Buffalo
1989	Brian Leetch, New York Rangers	Trevor Linden, Vancouver
1990	Sergei Makarov, Calgary	Mike Modano, Minnesota
1991	Ed Belfour, Chicago	Sergei Fedorov, Detroit

1992	Pavel Bure, Vancouver	Nicklas Lidstrom, Detroit
1993	Temu Selanne, Winnipeg	Joe Juneau, Boston
1994	Martin Brodeur, New Jersey	Jason Arnott, Edmonton
1995	Peter Forsberg, Quebec	Jim Carey, Washington
1996	Daniel Alfredsson, Ottawa	Eric Daze, Chicago
1997	Bryan Berard, New York Islanders	Jarome Iginla, Calgary

Conn Smythe Trophy
(most valuable player, Stanley Cup Playoffs)

1965 Jean Beliveau, Montreal
1966 Roger Crozier, Detroit
1967 Dave Keon, Toronto
1968 Glenn Hall, Toronto
1969 Serge Savard, Montreal
1970 Bobby Orr, Boston
1971 Ken Dryden, Montreal
1972 Bobby Orr, Boston
1973 Yvan Cournoyer, Montreal
1974 Bernie Parent, Philadelphia
1975 Bernie Parent, Philadelphia
1976 Reggie Leach, Philadelphia
1977 Guy Lafleur, Montreal
1978 Larry Robinson, Montreal
1979 Bob Gainey, Montreal
1980 Bryan Trottier, NY Islanders
1981 Butch Goring, NY Islanders
1982 Mike Bossy, NY Islanders
1983 Billy Smith, NY Islanders
1984 Mark Messier, Edmonton
1985 Wayne Gretzky, Edmonton
1986 Patrick Roy, Montreal
1987 Ron Hextall, Philadelphia
1988 Wayne Gretzky, Edmonton
1989 Al MacInnis, Calgary
1990 Bill Ranford, Edmonton
1991 Mario Lemieux, Pittsburgh
1992 Mario Lemieux, Pittsburgh
1993 Patrick Roy, Montreal
1994 Brian Leetch, NY Rangers
1995 Claude Lemieux, New Jersey
1996 Joe Sakic, Colorado
1997 Mike Vernon, Detroit
1998 Steve Yzeiman, Detroit

APPENDIX C
NHL Career Records
(* denotes active player)

Most Seasons
26 Gordie Howe
24 Alex Delvecchio
   Tim Horton
23 Johnny Bucyk
22 Dean Prentice
   Stan Mikita
   Doug Mohns

Most Goals
861 *Wayne Gretzky
801 Gordie Howe
731 Marcel Dionne
717 Phil Esposito
696 Mike Gartner

Highest Goals-per-Game Average
.823 Mario Lemieux
.767 Cy Denneny
.762 Mike Bossy
.717 *Brett Hull
.646 *Wayne Gretzky

Most Assists
1843 *Wayne Gretzky
1063 *Paul Coffey
1049 Gordie Howe
1040 Marcel Dionne
1001 *Ray Bourque

Highest Assists-per-Game Average
1.381 *Wayne Gretzky
1.183 Mario Lemieux

.982 Bobby Orr
.893 Adam Oates
.878 *Paul Coffey

Most Points

2705 *Wayne Gretzky
1850 Gordie Howe
1771 Marcel Dionne
1590 Phil Esposito
1552 *Mark Messier

Highest Points-per-Game Average

2.026 *Wayne Gretzky
2.005 Mario Lemieux
1.497 Mike Bossy
1.393 Bobby Orr
1.310 *Steve Yzerman

Most Penalty Minutes

3966 Dave Williams
3343 *Dale Hunter
3146 Tim Hunter
3078 *Marty McSorley
3043 Chris Nilan

Goaltending/Most Wins

477 Terry Sawchuk
434 Jacques Plante
423 Tony Esposito
407 Glenn Hall
355 Roger Vachon

APPENDIX D
NHL Single-Season Records

Most Goals

92	Wayne Gretzky, Edm.	1981–82
87	Wayne Gretzky, Edm.	1983–84
86	Brett Hull, St.L.	1990–91
85	Mario Lemieux, Pit.	1988–89
76	Phil Esposito, Bos.	1970–71
	Alexander Mogilny, Buf.	1992–93
	Teemu Selanne, Win.	1992–93

73	Wayne Gretzky, Edm.	1984–85
72	Brett Hull, St.L.	1989–90
71	Jarri Kurri, Edm.	1984–85
	Wayne Gretzky, Edm.	1982–83

Most Assists

163	Wayne Gretzky, Edm.	1985–86
135	Wayne Gretzky, Edm.	1984–85
125	Wayne Gretzky, Edm.	1982–83
122	Wayne Gretzky, L.A.	1990–91
121	Wayne Gretzky, Edm.	1986–87
120	Wayne Gretzky, Edm.	1981–82
118	Wayne Gretzky, Edm.	1983–84
114	Wayne Gretzky, Edm.	1988–89
	Mario Lemieux, Pit.	1988–89
109	Wayne Gretzky, Edm.	1980–81
	Wayne Gretzky, Edm.	1987–88

Most Points

215	Wayne Gretzky, Edm.	1985–86
212	Wayne Gretzky, Edm.	1981–82
208	Wayne Gretzky, Edm.	1984–85
205	Wayne Gretzky, Edm.	1983–84
199	Mario Lemieux, Pit.	1988–89
196	Wayne Gretzky, Edm.	1982–83
183	Wayne Gretzky, Edm.	1986–87
168	Wayne Gretzky, Edm.	1988–89
	Mario Lemieux, Pit.	1987–88
164	Wayne Gretzky, Edm.	1980–81

Most Penalty Minutes

472	Dave Schultz, Phil.	1974–75
409	Paul Baxter, Pit.	1981–82
408	Mike Peluso, Chi.	1991–92
405	Dave Schultz, L.A./Pit.	1977–78
399	Marty McSorley, L.A.	1992–93

Goaltending/Most Wins

47	Bernie Parent, Phil.	1973–74
44	Bernie Parent, Phil.	1974–75
	Terry Sawchuk, Det.	1950–51
	Terry Sawchuk, Det.	1951–52

43	Tom Barrasso, Pit.	1992–93		Ken Dryden, Mtl.	1975–76
	Ed Belfour, Chi.	1990–91	41	Ken Dryden, Mtl.	1976–77
42	Jacques Plante, Mtl.	1955–56			
	Jacques Plante, Mtl.	1961–62			

APPENDIX E
Members of the Hockey Hall of Fame

Forwards

Sid Abel
Jack Adams
Syl Apps
George Armstrong
Ace Bailey
Dan Bain
Bill Barber
Marty Barry
Andy Bathgate
Bobby Bauer
Jean Beliveau
Doug Bentley
Max Bentley
Toe Blake
Mike Bossy
Frank Boucher
George Boucher
Russell Bowie
Punch Broadbent
John Bucyk
Billy Burch
Dit Clapper
Bobby Clarke
Neil Colville
Charlie Conacher
Bill Cook
Bun Cook
Yvan Cournoyer
Bill Cowley
Rusty Crawford
Jack Darragh
Scotty Davidson
Hap Day
Alex Delvecchio

Cy Denneny
Marcel Dionne
Gord Drillon
Graham Drinkwater
Woody Dumart
Tommy Dunderdale
Babe Dye
Phil Esposito
Arthur Farrell
Frank Foyston
Frank Fredrickson
Bob Gainey
Jimmy Gardner
Boom Boom Geoffrion
Eddie Gerard
Rod Gilbert
Billy Gilmour
Shorty Green
Joe Hall
George Hay
Bryan Hextall
Tom Hooper
Gordie Howe
Syd Howe
Bobby Hull
Harry Hyland
Dick Irvin
Busher Jackson
Moose Johnson
Aurel Joliat
Duke Keats
Red Kelly
Ted Kennedy
Dave Keon
Elmer Lach
Guy Lafleur

Newsy Lalonde
Edgar Laprade
Jacques Lemaire
Herbie Lewis
Ted Lindsay
Mickey MacKay
Lanny McDonald
Frank McGee
Billy McGimsie
Frank Mahovlich
Joe Malone
Jack Marshall
Stan Mikita
Dickie Moore
Howie Morenz
Bill Mosienko
Frank Nighbor
Reg Noble
Buddy O'Connor
Harry Oliver
Bert Olmstead
Lynn Patrick
Gilbert Perreault
Tommy Phillips
Joe Primeau
Bob Pulford
Jean Ratelle
Henri Richard
Maurice Richard
George Richardson
Gordon Roberts
Blair Russell
Jack Ruttan
Fred Scanlan
Milt Schmidt
Sweeney Schriner

Oliver Seibert
Steve Shutt
Babe Siebert
Darryl Sittler
Alf Smith
Clint Smith
Hooley Smith
Tommy Smith
Barney Stanley
Nels Stewart
Bruce Stuart
Cyclone Taylor
Harry Trihey
Norm Ullman
Jack Walker
Marty Walsh
Harry E. Watson
Harry P. Watson
Cooney Weiland

Defensemen

Leo Boivin
Dickie Boon
Butch Bouchard
Buck Boucher
Harry Cameron
King Clancy
Sprague Cleghorn
Lionel Conacher
Art Coulter
Red Dutton
Fernie Flaman
Bill Gadsby
Herb Gardiner
Moose Goheen
Ebbie Goodfellow

Mike Grant
Doug Harvey
Red Horner
Tim Horton
Harry Howell
Ching Johnson
Tom Johnson
Jacques Laperriere
Guy Lapointe
Jack Laviolette
Sylvio Mantha
George McNamara
Bobby Orr
Brad Park
Lester Patrick
Pierre Pilote
Didier Pitre
Denis Potvin
Babe Pratt
Marcel Pronovost
Harvey Pulford
Bill Quackenbush
Ken Reardon
Larry Robinson
Art Ross
Borje Salming
Serge Savard
Earl Seibert
Eddie Shore
Joe Simpson
Allan Stanley
Black Jack Stewart
Hod Stuart
Gord Wilson

Rovers

Hobey Baker
Si Griffis
Fred Maxwell
Frank Rankin
Ernie Russell
Harry Westwick
Fredrick Whitcroft

Goalies

Clint Benedict
Johnny Bower
Frank Brimsek
Turk Broda
Gerry Cheevers
Alex Connell
Ken Dryden
Bill Durnan
Tony Esposito
Chuck Gardiner
Eddie Giacomin
George Hainsworth
Glenn Hall
Riley Hern
Hap Holmes
Bouse Hutton
Hughie Lehman
Percy LeSueur
Harry Lumley
Paddy Moran
Bernie Parent
Jacques Plante
Chuck Rayner
Terry Sawchuck
Billy Smith
Tiny Thompson
Vladislav Tretiak
Georges Vezina
Gump Worsley
Roy Worters

Builders

Charles F. Adams
Weston W. Adams
Frank Aheam
Bunny Ahearne
Sir Montagu Allan
Keith Allen
Al Arbour
Harold Ballard
Father David Bauer
J. P. Bickell
Scotty Bowman

George V. Brown
Walter A. Brown
Frank Buckland
Jack Butterfield
Frank Calder
Angus Campbell
Clarence Campbell
Joseph Cattarinich
Leo Dandurand
Frank Dilio
George Dudley
Jimmy Dunn
Alan Eagleson
Emile Francis
Jack Gibson
Tommy Gorman
Frank Griffiths
Bill Hanley
Charles Hay
Jim Hendy
Foster Hewitt
William Hewitt
Fred Hume
Punch Imlach
Tommy Ivan
Bill Jennings
Bob Johnson
Gordon Juckes
General Kilpatrick
Seymour Knox III
Al Leader
Bob LeBel
Tommy Lockhart
Paul Loicq
John Mariucci
Frank Mathers
Fredric McLaughlin
Jake Milford
Sen. Hartland Molson
Francis Nelson
Bruce Norris
James Norris
James D. Norris
William Northey
J. Ambrose O'Brien

Brian O'Neil
Fred Page
Frank Patrick
Allan Pickard
Rudy Pilous
Bud Polie
Sam Pollock
Sen. Donat Raymond
John Ross Robertson
Claude Robinson
Philip Ross
Glen Sather
Dr. Gunther Sebetzki
Frank Selke
Harry Sinden
Frank Smith
Conn Smythe
Ed Snider
Lord Stanley
James Sutherland
Anatoli Tarasov
Bill Torrey
Lloyd Turner
Thayer Tutt
Carl Voss
Fred Waghorne
Arthur Wirtz
Bill Wirtz
John Ziegler

Referees/Linesmen

Neil Armstrong
John Ashley
Bill Chadwick
John D'Amico
Chaucer Elliott
George Hayes
Bobby Hewitson
Mickey Ion
Matt Pavelich
Mike Rodden
Cooper Smeaton
Red Storey
Frank Udvari

For More Information

Books

Aretha, David. *The Montreal Canadiens Hockey Team.* Springfield, N.J.: Enslow, 1998.

Christopher, Matt. *On the Ice with Wayne Gretzky.* Boston: Little Brown, 1996.

Duplacey, James. *Amazing Forwards* (Hockey Superstars). New York: Beech Tree Books, 1996

Hunter, Douglas. *A Breed Apart: An Illustrated History of Goaltending.* Chicago: Triumph Books, 1996

———. *Champions: The Illustrated History of Hockey's Greatest Dynasties.* Chicago: Triumph Books, 1997.

Italia, Bob, and Paul Joseph. *100 Unforgettable Moments in Pro Hockey.* Minneapolis: Abdo & Daughters, 1998.

Knapp, Ron. *Top 10 Hockey Scorers.* Springfield, N.J.: Enslow, 1994.

Sullivan, George. *All About Hockey.* New York: Putnam, 1998.

Weekes, Don, and Kerry Banks. *Classic Hockey Trivia.* New York: Sterling, 1997.

For Advanced Readers

Brodeur, Denis, and Daniel Daignault. *Goalies: Guardians of the Net.* Toronto: Key Porter Books, 1996.

Fischler, Stan. *Illustrated History of Hockey.* Willowdale, Ontario: Warwick, 1993.

Leonetti, Mike, and Harold Barkley. *The Game We Knew: Hockey in the Fifties.* Vancouver: Raincoast Books, 1997.

McDonnell, Chris, ed. *For the Love of Hockey: Hockey Stars' Personal Stories.* Willowdale, Ontario: Firefly Books, 1997.

MacSkimming, Roy. *Cold War: The Amazing Canada-Soviet Hockey Series of 1972.* New York: Sterling, 1997.

Internet

http://www.lcshockey.com/
A peerless hockey site. Home of both a brash and funny weekly newsletter chronicling hockey events, and Hockey over Time, a mind-boggling archive of information and statistics about the game.

http://www.canoe.com/Hockey/home.html
Among the hockey pages at Slam! Sports, a large Web site devoted to Canadian sports, is coverage of recent NHL news and statistics; pages on all the junior and minor leagues; chat rooms; polls judging the NHL's most talented players and its toughest; and a great page on the long-gone World Hockey Association.

http://www.nhl.com
The official site of the National Hockey League is a central clearinghouse of hockey information, with links to official team sites, fan forums, and Stanley Cup history.

http://www.hhof.com
The official site of the Hockey Hall of Fame.

http://people.ne.mediaone.net/gilman/o6.html
A site dedicated to the Six-Team Era, which spanned the years 1942–67. Exhaustive summaries of each season, along with extensive statistics.

http://geocities.com/Colosseum/Track/5639/
A site that brings alive the dramatic, eight-game-long 1972 Summit Series between Canada and the Soviet Union. Audio files, articles, personal remembrances, and biographies of all the players and personalities involved.

Index

Page numbers in *italics* indicate illustrations.

About the Author

Mark Stewart ranks among the busiest sportswriters of the 1990s. He has produced hundreds of profiles on athletes past and present and authored more than 40 books, including biographies of Jeff Gordon, Monica Seles, Steve Young, Hakeem Olajuwon, and Cecil Fielder. A graduate of Duke University, he is currently president of Team Stewart, Inc., a sports information and resource company located in Monmouth County, New Jersey.